ESCHATOLOGICAL JUDGMENTS
A New Black Theology of the End Times
BLACK DIVINITY SERIES VOL 2

SHAHIDI ISLAM

Book Ordering Information
Cover design provided by: https://www.fiverr.com/patrick_2013
Email: shahidiislam@godbodyinternational.com
https://godbodyinternational.com

Attention African American Theologians!!!

Imagine the Beauties of Life Unfolded, the Wisdom of the Ages Revealed, and the Mysteries of God Come to Light

A Godbody Theology of the First Resurrection is the third instalment in Shahidi Islam's *Black Divinity Series*. Based on decades of research, see many of the truths distorted by years of slavery and colonialism now uncovered. To learn more shop now.

A Godbody Theology of the First Resurrection

This book is dedicated to the Gods and
Goddesses of the foundation,
who dwell in a Nation of love, peace, and
happiness

Table of Contents

Series Preface

The current *Black Divinity Series* was originally written to create a new kind of Black theology: a Black Godbody Theology. The starting point for this theology is that all Black people are divine, yet this concept of Black divinity actually has a long history. It was first articulated by the ancient Ethiopians over twenty-eight millennia ago, in a land that was called in times past Ta Neteru (the land of the gods and goddesses). The message was then continued on in ancient Egypt by the various mystical traditions, around another nine millennia ago; and by the ancient Hebrew mystical traditions over three millennia ago. The message was eventually lost to the Hebrews during their many exiles, but it was still maintained in ancient Egypt and ancient Ethiopia over the vast centuries.

Then came the Baptist to revive among the Judeans the understanding of Black divinity. He would also start a liberation movement among the Judeans, predicting the coming of someone after him, in his own lifetime, who would bring the people back to their Black divinity through a baptism into holiness and into a fully independent monarchy. The very Messiah he prophesied, would continue on that message, which after his disappearance splintered off into several separate branches.

The mystics among his followers were called the gnostics and they combined the Messiah's message with the ancient Egyptian philosophy. The gnostic message thereby continued the idea of Black divinity secretly and underground during a time when even the mainstream messianic movement was also underground (due mainly to heavy persecution). Unfortunately, when the messianic movement, finally, did gain legality it was only the mainstream version. Gnosticism, however, would remain an outlaw movement, thus driving them even further underground.

At that time, within the mainstream movement the only Black person considered truly divine was the Messiah (back then the only images of the Messiah were as a Black man). Black divinity then re-emerged with Islamic mysticism, a tradition that combined the gnostic oral tradition with Islamic interpretations of the Quran. The Prophet himself was an ardent follower of gnostic ideas and beliefs. It is even likely that he was trained and mentored by a practicing gnostic. Whether this is true or not, we know for sure that he referenced several gnostic teachings and traditions in the Quran that he could not have possibly known without having some familiarity with their history.

Finally, Black divinity would ultimately reach its greatest height in America, starting with the Honorable Elijah Muhammad bringing to the Black communities of America that Islamic mystical tradition through his Lost-Found Nation of Islam. From the Nation of Islam would then eventually emerge the godbody movement: a movement in the ghetto that went on to define G.O.D. as guns over drugs—thereby interpreting that the militant Black man that gains Knowledge 120 becomes a God in his own right, having the power to give life (through spreading 120) and to take life (we all know how); and to build; and to destroy.

Now for the most part we try to use this power, not to take life, but to build through it a Nation of Gods and Earths (hereafter to be called Goddesses).

That said, the 120 lessons we godbodies endorse are, again, only just the Supreme Wisdom lessons of the Honorable Elijah Muhammad. In that sense they have been read and mastered by several heroes and heroines within the Black community including: Minister Louis Farrakhan, Minister Malcolm X, Imam Warith Deen Muhammad, Dr. Khalid Muhammad, Dr. Sebi Alfredo Bowman, Dr. Malachi Z. York, the Champ Muhammad Ali, Erikah Badu, Bilal the 1st Born, D'Angelo, Jay Electronica, Busta Rhymes, Rakim Allah, Nas, Foxy Brown, Queen Latifah, all of the Fugees, the Wu-Tang Clan, Mobb Deep, and Brand Nubian. Even so, while the United States government has attacked and attempted to discredit many of these Black leaders, all of them are still well beloved by most Black people. The truth is, we Black people have always had the potential for divinity, but it is only now that we are starting to realise how to actually achieve it.

True, it may be currently accepted among the godbody – again, the ghetto organisation that is currently the central body propagating the message of Black divinity – that once a city, a nation, and the world comes to accept the truth of our destiny then a Black thearchy will begin to exist upon the earth. Indeed, as any true solarpunk/ecofuturist would much rather aim and strive for a low-tech and high-empath future; even so, within the godbody a more ghetto combination of solarpunk and Neo-Soul is believed to be more desirable; but that mainly through Black people taking their place as a God-Collective of the divine Black people we have always been.

Series Introduction

The current series is based on notes originally written in 2006 and edited in 2012 and again in 2019 for the purpose of liberating my people. Contained within are also a very large cross-section of quotations that break up a lot of the content making it seem at times frustrating and a little hard to read. This annoyance was unavoidable due to the current situation, and the unfortunate mistrust of those outside of the street life of the intelligence of anyone arising out of the street life. Again, hopefully no one within the street life, particularly within the Five Percent Nation, will be too offended by some of the language that I have chosen to use throughout, as it was mainly for the purpose of speaking to the uninitiated, not to ruin our image or desecrate our culture.

From an historical context all past developments in human progress have been correlated to philosophical precursors. From Aristotle's influence on ancient Greece and Plato's influence over the Roman *res publica*; to the influence of Rousseau on the French Revolution and Marx on the Russian; it is virtually impossible to separate historical epochs from their philosophical precursors. The initial philosophical bursts of light and hope, however, usually begin to dim as the pains of reaction begin to set in. This reactionary response to the new ideas and the hostility of its opposition usually bring great sorrow and disillusionment to the representatives of the new vision and ideal.

As these realities are the historical norm for all prior to revolutionary changes it is clear that anything of this calibre will meet also its own huge bursts of reactionary opposition and rage. From church pulpit to political gathering, from social clubs to cultural events all groups and sections of society claim allegiance to morality and against the dark cloud of the street life. True indeed, as the streets are considered a curse on society, and themselves cursed of God, we, in the eyes of those outside of the streets, should have nothing to do with anything even resembling the theocentric, let alone the thearchic. In fact, our anti-establishment makes us seem to any who are not affiliated to be more nihilistic than ritualistic. This anti-establishment being a product of our rejection by the establishment and being outcasts to it, has caused us to question our place in a society that would create and tolerate such vicious injustices as occur in the neighbourhoods of this so-called Western society.

But the Black thearchy itself is really just a system based on the identification of a new Black theodicy, that is, a study of God's goodness and righteousness from a Black person's perspective. Having arisen from the backstreets of New York as the godbody, we have taken their general outlook and message, and added to them theological, psychological, ideological, sociological, ecological, and cosmological depth. Conversely, though, the Black thearchy is primarily based on the use of godbody codes and culture to achieve Black identity amid the difficult and adverse situations of racism, poverty, humiliation, demonisation, dyseducation, discrimination, marginalisation, criminalisation, and state-orchestrated incarceration.

As a people most of we Blacks have been separated from our history and a knowledge of our history; but as Nature expresses herself through a cyclical rhythm of spontaneous repetitions, I feel that a knowledge of recent Black history is worth acknowledging. Marcus Garvey inspired an entire generation with the thought of a Black God. A God, not White like their slave-masters (or like their job-managers in this current system of wage-slavery) but a God Black like them, who understood the trials and sufferings of the people and offered them the strength and power to redeem themselves from these sufferings.

This philosophy spread in Africa, America, and the Caribbean in many forms. Two most obvious forms were the Rastafarians, who claimed Negusa Negast Tafari was the Black God incarnate, and the Black theologians, who claimed the Messiah Jesus was the Black God incarnate. But you also had the Black Muslims, who claimed Master Fard Muhammad was the Black God incarnate. Then you had the Afrocentrics who claimed the ancestral gods of Africa (particularly those of ancient Egypt), which manifest themselves in Nature, were the Black gods incarnate. Even the Kemetic scholars (who are commonly and derisively called "Hoteps" by most Black people) would claim the Egyptian god Ra to be the Black God incarnated in all Black males; similar to the Five Percent, who claim Allah to be *the God* incarnated in all Black males who have mastered the 120 lessons and opened the third eye of astral vision.

All that said, the basis for the current *Black Divinity Series* is six categorical systems which are instituted within the godbody movement to allow for our further continuance: Black divinity, Black revolutionism, Black eroticism, Black astralism, Black demodernisation, and Black syndicalism. These all effectively spell up to the words: Black DREADS; and all also make up the godbody ideology that I endorse —

and are generally accepted within the godbody movement as a whole – though they have never been spelled-out or outlined in this sort of way before. What I thereby hope to accomplish with this undertaking is a complete renewal of our movement and the lessons of the movement as handed down to me by my mentor and enlightener so as to show where our movement can lead and why the actual teleology of godbodyism will be a positive and not a self-destructive one.

In itself the godbody theory articulated throughout has been designed to be a form of Black ideology that incorporates ideas, language, and expressions from chaos theory, deconstruction theory, decolonising theory, post-colonial theory, critical race theory, pro-Black anarchist theory, and pro-sex womanist theory into the outlook and world vision of the Five Percent Nation. And as stated earlier the Five Percent Nation as a movement teaches that the Black man is God. Beginning in the 1960s under the leadership of a direct disciple of Malcolm X, who at that time was named Clarence 13X, but who we call Allah out of respect for the vision he received of the potential divinity of all Black men, obviously including himself, we seek also to enlighten our people as to their potential.

The traditions of the godbody movement founded by Allah are, again, based on the 120 lessons, which in themselves are really just the Supreme Wisdom lessons of the Honorable Elijah Muhammad. In that sense they have been read and mastered by several heroes and heroines within the Black community: Minister Louis Farrakhan, Minister Malcolm X, Imam Warith Deen Muhammad, Dr. Khalid Muhammad, Dr. Sebi Alfredo Bowman, Dr. Malachi Z. York, Muhammad Ali, Jay Electronica, Busta Rhymes, Erikah Badu, Ice Cube, Rakim Allah, Nas, Mobb Deep, the Wu-Tang Clan, and Brand Nubian. Furthermore, while the

United States government has attacked and attempted to discredit many of these Black leaders here mentioned, all of them are still well beloved by the Black community in general.

Nevertheless, my central cause for rewriting *Black Divinity* as a series was not just so as to create a new ideology and sociology for Black people, but more so to make a kind of ghetto theology, a Black Godbody Theology, for our overall empowerment. It cannot be denied that the godbody has a theology as we all share a general theory of God, of the devil, and of righteousness. Yet, as an African American theology the godbody theology can still be differentiated from that of the classical model of African American theology. If we take as an example the four degrees of faith (Skousen 2017): from no faith, to little faith, to great faith, to complete faith, we can see that classical African American theology features most of these four levels: the humanists have no faith, the liberationists/womanists have great faith, and the prosperous have complete faith. Well, we godbodies complete the cipher by having little faith, believing God to exist mainly in natural phenomena like a Universal Intelligence, the Universal Laws, the Original Black man, and all Original people.

Basically, it is the aim and purpose of this book to represent the godbody movement by, firstly, seeking to introduce the godbody theology as an African American theology nuanced from Cone's in that it is not a survival theology but a thrival theology; a thrival theology that came out of the ghetto experience to give to the Black people of the ghetto the hope for a better future, one which they themselves create. Herein, Black Godbody Theology is a ghetto theology that promotes Black improvement and empowerment; even as James Cone himself stated, "Unless theology can become 'ghetto theology,' a theology that speaks to black people, the gospel message has no promise of life for the black man – it is a lifeless message" (Cone 2021: 37).

Even so, it must obviously also be noted that a lot of the ideas and practices encouraged throughout are not those of the entire godbody of the United States, but are add-ons I developed based on lessons I learned in the Socialist Workers Party as an anti-capitalist and in the Black Church as a Pentecostal. As I left America as a "newborn" godbody I never had the chance to fully master the 120 lessons; I did, however, take a lot of the lessons I learned in cipher with the godbody and expound on them to co-create with my enlightener: God Born Supreme Allah, a Black thearchy based on his own GBSA-ideology. This book therefore is mainly a union of all the previous movements I learned from so as to contribute to the further empowering of our people.

Recognising also that a lot of the Gods themselves have no tolerance for innovation; I concluded that we stand no hope of ever overthrowing White supremacy without making certain changes to our lessons. We will never elevate until we are willing to innovate. And if we were to find that something was emphatically wrong we would be obliged to destroy it and so elevate beyond it, even as we destroy the mathematics of anyone who does not backup their lessons with proof. It is my hope that these lessons, which are mainly based on quotations, can be used by all other newborns to understand how the Gods build, and by godbodies to bring us to a place of true divinity in our ways and actions based on knowledge, wisdom, and under-standing. True indeed, as the highest form of understanding is love, even so, the highest form of love is libidinal, it is by this kind of love that we will be able to elevate beyond local hood heroes to become global superheroes.

Finally, it is my intention for the current approach to be used to inform the course of the godbody movement in its rise to popularity, and to create an avenue for the acceptance of this theological perspective within the current discussions of African American theology. Within this context I pay homage to those who came before me in the classical schools: Anthony B. Pinn, William R. Jones, James H. Cone, Albert B. Cleage, Delores S. Williams, Kelly B. Douglas, Robert S. Beckford, Anthony G. Reddie, Creflo A. Dollar, and Thomas D. Jakes. Still, it must also be said at this point that although I am myself a fellow of the Society for the Study of Theology, all the ideas and outlooks presented in this book are overwhelmingly my own and nobody else's. Peace.

The Supreme Mathematics

Potentials

k = knowledge (1)

w = wisdom (2)

u = understanding (3)

f = freedom – I choose not to add culture as freedom is the most obvious elevation from understanding and culture is implied in the whole mathematics (4)

p = power – (I use the term power neither in the Marxian sense, as in to dominate nor in the Foucauldian sense, as in to discipline or surveille; but instead use it in the Adlerian sense as in empowerment) I choose not to add refinement as power is the next elevation from freedom and progresses till it reaches equality (5)

e = equality (6)

G = God – where God is equivalent to the omnipresent, and not to a state of pure perfection (7)

B = build – when adding on (8)

D = destroy – when subtracting (8)

$\forall$ = born (9)

$\circ$ = cipher (0)

Symbols

D = dialectical moment where *pa* > *na* becomes *na* > *pa*, or vice versa.

Lm = the limitation

$\exists$ = when there is

$+$ = together with

$\in$ = the sum includes

$>$ = greater than

$\geq$ = greater than or equal to

$<$ = lesser then

$\leq$ = lesser than or equal to

$\rightarrow$ = leads on to

$\leftrightarrow$ = if and only if

$\nearrow$ = on the increase

$\searrow$ = on the decrease

$\propto$ = proportional to

Values

∞ = infinity

o = zero

λ = wavelength

A = amplitude

d = displacement

t = time expended

v = rate of velocity

δ = astral forces $->x^1$

α = social forces $->x^{10}$

β = global forces $->x^{20}$

θ = environmental forces $->x^{30}$

ϕ = terrestrial forces (also called geomagnetic forces) $->x^{40}$

ϑ = solar forces (also called heliospheric magnetic forces) $->x^{50}$

∂ = globular forces (also called stellar magnetic forces) $->x^{60}$

φ = galactic forces (also called galactic magnetic forces) $->x^{70}$

ψ = super-clusteral forces (also called intercluster magnetic forces) $->x^{80}$

$\mathcal{E}$ = cosmic forces $->x^{90}$

Pa = positive action of an individual

pa = positive action of a social body

Na = negative action of an individual

na = negative action of a social body

x = social potential of a social body

n = level of social potentiality

g = a social movement

$opp.g$ = an oppressing social movement

$emp.g$ = an empowering social movement

(pa) = all the positive actions of a social body

(na) = all the negative actions of a social body

(v) = all the social velocity

(g) = the whole social movement

S = decelerative force caused by reaction of social body x_1

R = accelerative force caused by resistance of social body x_2

S = syndicalism

The Godbody System

The Universal Laws of Existence

1. The law of interaction (whose corollary is the pleasure principle),

2. The law of intersubjectivity (whose corollary is the vibratory law),

3. The law of self-organisation (whose corollary is the identity law),

4. The law of opposition (whose corollary is the polarity law),

5. The law of repetition (whose corollary is the inertia law),

6. The law of self-similarity (whose corollary is the correspondence law),

7. The law of conservation (whose corollary is the reciprocity law),

8. The law of evolution (whose corollary is the power law),

9. The law of devolution (whose corollary is the entropy law),

10. The law of self-destruction (whose corollary is the phase-transition law),

11. The law of interconnectivity (whose corollary is the synchronicity law), and

12. The law of interrelation (whose corollary is the eternalist law).

The 10 Principles

1. No God but Allah

2. No power imbalances

3. No non-authors

4. No non-fighters

5. No Divine fights alone

6. No problems handled in the Square should ever leave the Square

7. No marriage or marriages

8. No missing parliament meetings

9. No wearing underwear

10. No harassment or rape of any kind ever

What We Teach

1. That Black people are the Original people of the planet earth.

2. That Black people are the fathers and mothers of civilization.

3. That the science of Supreme Mathematics is the key to understanding man's relationship to the universe.

4. That Islam is a natural way of life, not a religion.

5. That education should be fashioned to enable us to be self sufficient as a people.

6. That each one should teach one according to their knowledge.

7. That the Black man is god and his proper name is ALLAH. Arm, Leg, Leg, Arm, Head.

8. That our children are our link to the future and they must be nurtured, respected, loved, protected and educated.

9. That the unified Black family is the vital building block of the nation.

The Hedgehog Concept (The Build Allah Square)

1. Eat, Train, Read, Write, and Share

The Core Concepts

1. Black divinity, Black revolutionism, Black eroticism, Black astralism, Black demodernisation, and Black syndicalism

The Physical Concepts

1. biophysics, quantum physics, molecular physics, geophysics, astrophysics, and digital physics

The Discursive Concepts

1. body, embody, and disembody

2. structure, infrastructure, and superstructure

3. subtle, subaltern, and subterranean

4. text, pretext, subtext, and context

5. discourse, discursive, pre-discursive, narrative, and performative

6. reality, surreality, sub-reality, hyper-reality, virtual-reality, and unreality

7. erase, absent, present, represent, reproduce, re-enact, legitimate, and counter

8. position, supposition, disposition, composition, superposition, opposition, exposition, and imposition

9. silence, distort, fabricate, exaggerate, implicate, explicate, delineate, propagate, and voice

The Chronological Concepts

1. historicism and historicity

2. linear-chronological and event-sequential

3. historical, ahistorical, prehistorical, and transhistorical

The Pneumatological Concepts

1. demonise and transfigure

2. divine, vampyre, and devil

3. elemental, environmental, and universal

4. foresight, insight, and hindsight

5. *Sebi*, *Nebi*, and *Obi*

6. astral, astral body, astral force, and astral plane

7. *Hakim*, *Karim*, *Rahim*, and Allah

8. Horu construct, Hethor construct, Ausar conscious, and Auset conscious

9. existent, pre-existent, co-existent, de-existent, and re-existent

10. resurrected, incorporated, *phantomised*, internalised, and exorcised

11. empathic, psychopathic, sociopathic, *monopathic, duopathic, polypathic,* and *panopathic*

12. empath, dark empath, supernova empath, true empath, quiet empath, psychic empath, super empath, sigma empath, and Heyoka empath

The Psychological Concepts

1. conscious and unconscious

2. libido and superego

3. inhibition, prohibition, and exhibitionism

4. object, selfobject, and objectify

5. subject, subjective, and intersubjective

6. trauma, complex, and therapy

7. power, empower, internalise, incorporate, and concretise

8. spectre, drive, constraint, ideal, and somatic

The Ideological Concepts

1. seduction, perverse seduction, and seductionism

2. sexualise, racialise, and criminalise

3. White superiority, White supremacy, and White privilege

4. acculturate, assimilate, integrate, and institutionalise

5. gaze, oppress, problematise, and deviate

6. shackling, unshackling, deshackling, and reshackling

7. typical, atypical, prototypical, and archetypal

8. institution, destitution, restitution, constitution, deconstitution, and reconstitution

9. sexual, asexual, heterosexual, homosexual, transsexual, intersexual, and hypersexual

10. modern, premodern, postmodern, late modern (liquid modern), anti-modern, and demodernise

11. colony, market-colony, industrial-colony, military-colony, penal-colony, settler-colony, spatial-colony, cultural-colony, corporeal-colony, mental-colony, epistemic-colony, counter-colony, neo-colony, and the Great United States Empire (GUSE)

The Sociological Concepts

1. embodied displacement (exile, migration, trans-migration, or tourism) and disembodied displacement (phantasy, fantasy, wish, dream, vision, imagination, or astral journey)

2. aetiology, teleology, and eschatology

3. locality, globality, and communality

4. ordination, subordination, and superordination

5. gnosis, prognosis, diagnosis, and epignosis

6. inertia, action, interaction (force), and act-species

7. interior, exterior, anterior, posterior, and ulterior

8. mechanic, elastic, static, kinetic, and dynamic

9. politics, geopolitics, biopolitics, necropolitics, transpolitics, hyper-politics, body-politics, racial-politics, and sexual-politics

The Sociological Axioms

1. The Axioms of Social Mechanics

a) $x > 1$

b) $v < 670{,}616{,}629$ mph

c) $v = \dfrac{d}{t}$

2. The Axioms of Social Force

a) $v\left(\dfrac{x^n}{x^n}\right) = \alpha$

b) $x_1 + R = Lm$ and $x_2 + S = Lm$

c) $\alpha > x^{10}$

3. The Axioms of Social Movements

a) $x_1 > x_2 \leftrightarrow x_2 \alpha \searrow 0$

b) $g \propto \alpha$

c) $g_1(pa) \rightarrow g_2(na)$ and $g_1(na) \rightarrow g_2(pa)$

d) $d = (2\pi) \times \left(\frac{2\lambda + 2A}{2}\right)$

4.   The Axioms of Social Kinetics

a) $x_1 + x_2 \rightarrow na$

b) $x_1 + x_2 \rightarrow pa \leftrightarrow Lm \searrow$

c) $pa > Lm \rightarrow D \leftrightarrow pa \searrow$

5.   The Axioms of Social Statics

a) $g(Lm) \leftrightarrow \alpha \searrow o$

b) $\exists \alpha \searrow o \rightarrow x^u \geq g$

6.   The Axioms of Social Dynamics

a) $Lm > g$

b) $\exists (\alpha > Lm) \rightarrow g \nearrow$

c) $\exists Lm \rightarrow \alpha \searrow + g \searrow$

Preface to Book

The book you are about to read focuses primarily on presenting to the reader the depths of certain godbody structures and ideas, using *observant participation* (Wacquant 2008) as its primary source. In particular it centres on godbody lessons that I learned during my experiences in both Brooklyn, New York and London, England, and the guidance I was given from my mentor and enlightener within the godbody movement. A man who himself is currently doing time in prison for a crime he did not commit.

The book was also written as part of a much broader book, carrying with it the central purpose of representing the New York City street culture and revealing some of its remarkable ideas to the Black intelligentsia of America. However, as I found it ever more difficult to get a footing in this crowd and among this audience I decided to rethink my original plan. Finding instead a home among African professionals I considered it far more necessary to remove some of the more immature and gang related themes of the original content and repackage it as a theology. My main objective at this time, at least with the current endeavour, is now to expound in detail the various aspects of this unique ghetto movement. A movement that has created a cultural mechanism so effective that it has changed the face and shape of the ghetto youth of the American East Coast and Black American underclass to this very day.

The primary focus of this particular book, however, is expounding on the subject of the last days, which in itself is a subject that is very intriguing and hotly debated. Questions like: when will the Second Coming of the Messiah be? Will the Messiah reign in Israel, Arabia, or America? What keeps, and has kept, the Second Coming from happening? Will there actually be a Millennial Reign? And all other questions about the *eschaton* (last things) have baffled countless theologians. While, true indeed, I myself cannot claim any superiority to these, I do belong to a tradition that has a novel way of answering these questions. In order to explain that tradition, however, I will have to start by explaining that from the early twentieth century three distinct traditions have emerged within the Black community: the Charismatic, the realistic, and the Islamic. This book will attempt to delineate an interpretation derived from the third but still maintain the novel perspective spoken of earlier.

That said, the three central Black eschatological traditions each have their own genealogy. The Charismatic can be traced back to Margaret Macdonald, through to the Plymouth Brethren, continuing on to William Seymour, and going on into Thomas D. Jakes Sr. At the same time, the realistic tradition began with Rudolf Bultmann, through to Reinhold Niebuhr, continuing on to Martin L. King Jr., and going on to James H. Cone. Then again, the Islamic tradition of Black eschatology began with Noble Drew Ali, through to W. D Fard Muhammad, continuing on to the Honorable Elijah Muhammad, and going on into the godbody movement. The reason I have chosen to end the Islamic tradition with the godbody movement instead of with the far more internationally credible Louis Farrakhan is that the movement I myself represent is the godbody which itself has a credibility all its own especially with the millions influenced by one of its more famous members like Nas, or Rakim, or Erikah Badu.

Finally, this book, as with all the books of this series, was mainly written to spread the message of my Sun and Enlightener: God Born Supreme Allah, and as a thank you to him for the jewels he dropped on me. These jewels effectively brought me to the light of truth and to the knowledge of myself. And to all the Gods and Earths out there, peace – coming straight from the God Shahidi Islam.

General Introduction

The epistle of Revelation is a very prophetic book. Written by the apostle John while on Patmos Island, it contains what most people believe to be the road map for the last days of the universe, or at least of humanity's existence in the universe. In order to understand some of the inherent symbologies behind these early traditions of messianism, and the mysticism of what physicists call phase-space, we will be venturing into a school of thought quite alien to most Westernised thinkers. Perhaps the best place to begin in this new school of thought is with the basic premise of all faith traditions: "It is by our faith that we know what we believe in will happen, being completely assured of a reality that is invisible" (Hebrews 11:1 my rewording).

Again, in ancient Egypt they had no problem with the idea of an invisible realm that only the third eye could tap into. A realm that we currently call the astral plane. Within this plane dwell as much of the deity's many manifold manifestations as within the physical, if not more. The obvious question from here then would be: if an invisible and basically astral realm exists where is the proof of its existence? Naturally, we godbodies understand that the symbolisms of the epistle of Revelation are just that: symbols. Yet we also see them as representing an interaction between astral, causal, and physical planes. With this understanding in mind we acknowledge that the epistle of Revelation has not yet been fulfilled, however, we also attempt to show and prove that the terrible plagues spoken of within it need never happen. To large sections within the godbody movement of the street life, judgment can be averted through respecting the life and teachings of Muhammad, Jesus, and the Prophets.

That said, the current book will not be dealing with everything written in the epistle of Revelation: that would take a book of far greater size to deal with. This book intends to simply limit its range to the judgments spoken of at the opening of the seals of the great book of Allah. It shall also hopefully show the relation and correlation between the prophecies in the epistle of the Revelation and those in the book of the Prophets. This will thereby prove, not only a continuity, but even a remedy for the current complacency within the world of today towards ethical righteousness. Allah can change his mind, he can change his word, he can even change his laws; but Allah can never change his nature. He is the same yesterday, today, and forever. It is even written in Hebrews concerning him, "Thou, Lord, in the beginning hast laid the foundation of the earth; and the heavens are the works of thine hands: They shall perish; but thou remainest; and they shall wax old as doth a garment; And as a vesture shalt thou fold them up, and they shall be changed: but thou art the same, and thy years shall not fail."

Three things must be mentioned, however, from the outset of this expedition, each articulated by biblical Theologian Marcus Maxwell in his commentary on Revelation. First of all, "the book of Revelation would have been perfectly well understood by the first century readers, and therefore [was] not a detailed blueprint of the plan of God for the Second Coming. It primarily addresses the churches of the Roman province of Asia Minor," so it should not to be interpreted to mean that everything must or will happen exactly as was written by the apostle John, nor that their fulfilment was merely a last days thing and not a very current, in the moment thing.

Secondly, "John recounts the same events several times, expanding the detail and providing fresh viewpoints. For instance, there are three series of seven judgments: the seals (beginning in chapter 6), the trumpets (from chapter 8), and the bowls (chapter 16). At first sight these are successive events but on closer examination turn out to be different perspectives on the same thing, since all end at the last judgment." The epistle is basically telling the same story seven times and in seven different cycles (if one counts as cycles the seven opening messages and the seven later thunders); thus by studying any one of these cycles we should, generally speaking, be able to understand the whole Revelation.

The third thing we must understand about the epistle of Revelation before we proceed is that based on the eschatology of it. Maxwell said on this matter, "In recent years some scholars have begun to argue that the images of cataclysmic change in apocalyptic language are not really about 'the end of the world.' Instead, they should be seen as predicting, or even calling for, great changes in the social order." "It seems to me that to a great extent, both views can be held together."

Prior to the first advent of the Messiah the prophets taught the people about ethical living, crying out to the people of Israel, Judea, and of the whole of the Middle East, telling them to administer justice and practice ethics. The prophet Isaiah, who was called by many the Prince of the Prophets, was, in his own day, the leader of a Prophetic School in Judea. It was here that he prepared others to preach a message of justice and the fear of the Lord. The prophet Isaiah cried out in those days to these, at that time, corrupted Judean people, saying, "None calleth for justice, nor any pleadeth for truth: they trust in vanity, and speak lies; they conceive mischief, and bring forth iniquity." At the same time, other prophets and contemporaries of the prophet Isaiah, raised their own rallying cry against corruption, saying: If "He is a merchant, the balances of deceit are in his hand: he loveth to oppress. And Ephraim said, Yet I am become rich, I have found me out substance: in all my labours they shall find none iniquity in me that were sin". "And I said, Hear, I pray you, O heads of Jacob, and ye princes of the house of Israel; Is it not for you to know judgment? Who hate the good, and love the evil".

We can therefore understand from here and elsewhere that a Black astralism can reveal to the world the genuine righteousness of Allah; that Allah pleads the cause of the poor and vulnerable people of society. So we can see that, even from ancient times, they had a better understanding of the reality and cause for fear over the imminent "Day of the Lord" spoken of by all the ancient prophets with fear and trembling. For the wrath of Allah is manifested against humanity for all their corrupted ways and all their corrupted views and all their corrupted lies. Wherefore the imagery used in the epistle of Revelation was simply a graphic and symbolic depiction of social and astral realities: not the fantastic use of an illusionary narrative.

Obviously, other prophetic voices also spoke of this situation in a little bit more detail. The prophet Joel said during the time of the Neo-Persian Empire, "Blow ye the trumpet in Zion, and sound an alarm in my holy mountain: let all the inhabitants of the land tremble: for the day of the Lord cometh, for it is nigh at hand; A day of darkness and of gloominess, a day of clouds and of thick darkness, as the morning spread upon the mountains: a great people and a strong; there hath not been ever the like, neither shall be any more after it, even to the years of many generations." This army which was here gathered across the mountains had clearly gathered for the purpose of war. But what are they warring for and who are they warring against? From the Revelation we can get an idea: they were warring to, simply put, conquer; and they were warring against the people of Israel.

Yet the prophets said concerning their battle:

"And the remnant of Jacob shall be among the Gentiles in the midst of many peoples as a lion among the beasts of the forest, as a young lion among the flocks of sheep: who, if he go through, both treadeth down, and teareth in pieces, and none can deliver. Thine hand shall be lifted up upon thine adversaries, and all thine enemies shall be cut off."

And "I will make Jerusalem a cup of trembling unto all the people round about, when they shall be in the siege both against Judah and against Jerusalem. And in that day will I make Jerusalem a burdensome stone for all people: all that burden themselves with it shall be cut in pieces, though all the people of the earth be gathered together against it. … And the governors of Judah shall say in their heart, The inhabitants of Jerusalem shall be my strength in the Lord of hosts their God. In that day will I make the governors of Judah like an hearth of fire among the wood, and like a torch of fire in a sheaf; and they shall devour all the people round about, on the right hand and on the left: and Jerusalem shall be inhabited again in her own place, even in Jerusalem. The Lord also shall save the tents of Judah first, that the glory of the house of David and the glory of the inhabitants of Jerusalem do not magnify themselves against Judah."

All this being a picture painted that gives the impression of a coming battle or warfare, one that, though appearing to be a political upheaval or conflict, may in actual fact be only a symbolic or figurative conflict. The reality of this view, though not yet very convincing, is given another thrashing by the prophet Ezekiel when he said quite plainly in his own astral journey: "And the word of the Lord came unto me, saying, Son of man, set thy face against Gog, the land of Magog, the chief prince of Meshech and Tubal, and prophesy against him, And say, Thus saith the Lord God; … After many days thou shalt be visited: in latter years thou shalt come into the land that is brought back from the sword, and is gathered out of many people, against the mountains of Israel, which have been always waste: but it is brought forth out of the nations, and they shall dwell safely all of them. Thou shalt ascend and come like a storm, thou shalt be like a cloud to cover the land, thou, and all thy bands, and many people with thee." All these words employed, essentially used the war imagery also employed by the prophet Joel, which themselves were employed so as to be an inspiration to his people.

From here we are also able to see the harsh realities of Allah bringing his thearchy to the earth, not the delusional fantasy of instant beauty and peace. Indeed, the Messiah himself said, "Think not that I am come to send peace on earth: I came not to send peace, but a sword." And again, "And a mighty angel took up a stone like a great millstone, and cast it into the sea, saying, Thus with *violence* shall that great city Babylon be thrown down" (17: 21; emphasis mine). Whereby, just like with the "Day of the Lord" in most Judean minds, so with the "Second Coming" of the Messiah in most Gentile minds; heavily romanticised, whitewashed, and infantilised by its "prophets." For someone to come along and destroy every worldly power and authority is for someone to come along and viscerally destroy everything that the world stands for, believes in, and has held to be most sacred.

The ultimate triumph of the Black thearchist movement thus will not come as a result of godbodies saying the right words or being absolutely perfect in every way. The fact of the matter is, a person has a better chance of converting real people by being their real imperfect selves, not by trying to put on an over moral show. This lesson even goes doubly for those who eschew morality and just desire to engage in the sexual pleasures of having seduced the unseducible: the most perfect seductions are imperfect and invalidated. That is because it is in those moments that appear as though a person is unmoved and unwilling to yield that their memory system kicks in, through which the depths of Allah's essence can be revealed to them. Hence we here need to, of necessity, not necessarily relearn all the early messianic symbols, at least not yet anyway, but to explore the judgments expressed in the revealed drama concerning the execution of Allah's wrath, and our averting it.

All this is where the theological meets the thearchical. For in the fifth chapter of Revelation we find the unravelling of a heavenly crescendo of praise, in which the symbolic Lamb figure was found worthy of that which was found at the right hand of the heavenly throne, and in its Greek variation was given the name the *Biblion*. It was the opening (or unsealing) of this *Biblion* that brought about the manifestation or realisation of all the apocalyptic cataclysms that followed.

More Than Conquerors

At the opening of the first seal (6: 1, 2) a white horse and its horseman appeared before the apostle John and the four living creatures that stood before the twenty-four seats, each one seated with one of twenty-four elders (elders that we in the godbody call: twenty-four Scientists). This horseman, at the time, was holding a bow, and was then given a crown and told that he was to go out, conquer, and overcome the world. We find later on that this very one sent out to conquer and overcome, may in fact have been an allusion to the very Messiah who – in 19: 11-16 – leads the armies of heaven, also riding upon white horses. In order to fully explain this paradox Maxwell made clear concerning the epistle of Revelation that "there are repetitions, visions within visions, and themes that seem to disappear only to reemerge later." The truth is, the events written in the epistle of Revelation, like all events that transpire in the astral plane, did not actualise in any linear fashion from one event to the next. Or, as Koester said, "visionary time has no straightforward connection to chronological time".

Such things are also true within our current dream worlds. Time in a dream may not necessarily move forward, and events can occur or reverse as the dream progresses; this is especially the case with the epistle of Revelation. Still, I see the rider of the white horse as the messianic hope actualised as opposed to Maxwell's theory of him being an imperial conqueror. The main reason for this is that the heathen do not rage until a light has first come to them, and "the Lord God does nothing before first revealing his mysteries to his servants the prophets" (my rewording).

To get to the bottom of all this we might need to venture into one of the influences the apostle John probably considered when envisioning, or at least when writing, his epistle of Revelation, the apocalypse of 2Esdras:

> *"And it came to pass after seven days, I dreamed a dream by night: And, lo, there arose a wind from the sea, that it moved all the waves thereof. And I beheld, and, lo, that man waxed strong with the thousands of heaven: and when he turned his countenance to look, all the things trembled that were seen under him. And whensoever the voice went out of his mouth, all they burned that heard his voice, like as the earth faileth when it feeleth the fire. And after this I beheld, and, lo, there was gathered together a multitude of men, out of number, from the four winds of the heaven, to subdue the man that came out of the sea. … And, lo, as he saw the violence of the multitude that came, he neither lifted up his hand, nor held sword, nor any instrument of war: But only I saw that he sent out of his mouth as it had been a blast of fire, and out of his lips a flaming breath, and out of his tongue he cast out sparks and tempests. And they were all mixed together; the blast of fire, the flaming breath, and the great tempest; and fell with violence upon the multitude which was prepared to fight, and burned them up every one, so that upon a sudden of an innumerable multitude nothing was to be perceived, but only dust and smell of smoke: when I saw this I was afraid" (2Esdras 13: 1-11).*

It is undeniable the influence this apocalyptic work had on the apostle John, for as he would go on to write in his own apocalyptic work: "And I will give power unto my two witnesses, and they shall prophesy a thousand two hundred and threescore days, clothed in sackcloth. These are the two olive trees and the two candlesticks standing before the God of the earth. And if any man will hurt them, fire proceedeth out of their mouth, and devoureth their enemies: and if any man will hurt them, he must in this manner be killed" (11: 3-5). And just in case you are unable to see here the relation between these two Scriptures and the rider on the white horse, the Messiah himself said concerning his message that "this gospel of the kingdom shall be preached in all the world for a witness unto all nations; and then shall the end come." Before the end can come Allah must first send out his witnesses to speak the message of thearchism; and when this begins to happens then know that judgment will soon follow.

To complete this very basic explication I will now turn to the prophet Zechariah, when he said, "then answered I, and said unto him, What are these two olive trees upon the right side of the candlestick and upon the left side thereof? And I said again, and said unto him, What be these two olive branches which through the two golden pipes empty the golden oil out of themselves? And he answered me and said, Knowest thou not what these be? And I said, No, my lord. Then said he, These are the two anointed ones, that stand by the Lord of the whole earth." All leading us to the interpretation that the two witnesses are in fact two messiahs who will be opposed by the people of this world when they share their witness of the thearchy. However, it may actually prove to be a little more complicated than that. The Hebrew word used by the prophet Zechariah in the above Scripture was not *mashiakh* (as in Messiah), but the word *yitshar*, which actually meant oil producers; yet I will here be translating it as little messiahs.

Thus, the rider of the white horse is not the Messiah as such, but is instead symbolic of the two witnesses, even as was said later on in the Revelation, "And the armies which were in heaven followed him upon white horses, clothed in fine linen, white and clean" (19: 14). Moreover, it also continued concerning the two witnesses, "these have power to shut heaven, that it rain not in the days of their prophecy: and have power over waters to turn them to blood, and to smite the earth with *all plagues*, as often as they will. And when they shall have finished their testimony, the beast that ascendeth out of the bottomless pit shall make war against them, and shall overcome them, and kill them" (11: 6, 7; emphasis mine).

Now for the record, the word used in this Scripture for witnesses was *martys*, which itself is rooted in the word *martyr*. Basically, the two witnesses are, or were supposed to be, two martyrs. What, however, is truly different about them is that they have the power to "smite the earth with all plagues as often as they will." As the Revelation was written to be predictive specifically of the *eschaton* (last things), the plagues called forth by the two witnesses must be understood to be the seven last plagues of the wrath of Allah (16: 1-21) – seven itself obviously being a symbolic number as the two witnesses may have a virtually limitless number of plagues they can call forth and bring forth upon the world. Therefore Revelation 16 provides a template of the kind of plagues the two witnesses may call forth – sores; turning seas into blood; turning rivers and fountains of water into blood; power over the sun; turning the Beast's kingdom to darkness; drying up the Euphrates to prepare the world for Armageddon; and earthquakes, thunderings, and great hail.

What is of extra interest is that there is also a relation between the seven vials and the seven trumpets. The first trumpet and the first vial affect the earth. The second trumpet and second vial affect the seas. The third trumpet and third vial affect the rivers and fountains of water. The fourth trumpet and fourth vial affect the sun. The fifth trumpet and fifth vial cause darkness to fill the land. The sixth trumpet and sixth vial affect the Euphrates. The seventh trumpet and seventh vial cause earthquakes, thunderings, voices, and great hail. In this instance, rather than look at all these plagues individually I shall simply say that the first five trumpets and first five vials could be interpreted to coincide with, and result from, the first seal – and the coming of the two witnesses.

Conversely, it could now further be asked why these two witnesses or two martyrs are here considered to be two little messiahs and not in fact the Messiah and his bride? The answer is that the two witnesses are destined to die "where also our Lord was crucified" (11: 8). Again, "Wherefore they are no more twain, but one flesh. What therefore God hath joined together, let not man put asunder." What we see from these two Scriptures is that the two witnesses are very likely to not be symbolic of the true Messiah that was crucified, but of a little messiah: or in this case a Great Witness. Besides, it makes more sense if it is a little messiah and not the Divine Parousia (divine advent) itself, as that may turn out relatively different.

The witness that comes thereby carries within himself or herself, the last plagues of Allah, because in him or her is filled up the wrath of Allah. Moreover, when he or she has finished their testament he or she shall then be martyred (killed) for having martyred (testified) their message. So then, what will their message be? To be sure, it will not be "For God so loved the world," which carries neither wrath, nor plague, nor judgment. It will thereby be a message, not of salvation, but of redemptive vengeance. Again, why should we believe in and fight for redemptive vengeance? This is a good question: the answer is most likely that the blood of the prophets and of the righteous people of the earth who died unjustly, and all the suffering endured by the victims of any iniquity or inequity, has been crying out to Allah from the time of the Renaissance to this day. Basically, the days of vengeance come when the witness brings down the wrath of Allah on humanity, thus bringing down the great *eschaton*. Finally, this dramatic tale, or group of tales, will all lead inexorably to the great deliverance of the righteous when the Messiah comes again to destroy the mythical Beast character at the very end of the world.

Again, this Beast character – though he was a borrowed symbol from the scroll of Daniel – who was himself personified in the Islamic traditions as the Great *Dajjal*, within the context of the vision and astral journey of the epistle of Revelation represented an opponent who was to fight against the Great Witness and ultimately bring about his or her actual death. Within certain Islamic sources it is even claimed that the Prophet said concerning the witness (who he considered to be a male), '"At that time a man who is the best of people – or from the best of people – will come and say to him, "I bear witness that you are indeed the Dajjaal, whom the Messenger of Allah … spoke to us about." The Dajjaal will say, "Suppose I kill this (man) and then bring him back to life. Will you then doubt about the matter." The people present will say, "No." He will kill him and then revive him, and upon being revived the (righteous) man will say, "By Allah, I have never understood you (and your situation) more clearly than I do now." The Dajjaal will then want to kill him, but he will not be given power over him.' (*Muslim*) Abu Ishaaq said, 'It is said that that man is Khidr.'"

Effectively, the Witness, based on various Near Eastern traditions, particularly Islamic ones, was to be a man of al-Khidr (in Arabic, the Black one: or literally, the green one), an acknowledged guide to the prophet Moses during his time in Arabia, that was in time believed to be one that would bear witness against the Great *Dajjal* (the Imposter). Al-Khidr itself, in Arabic and Islamic sources, was considered to be a tribal grouping in Arabia. The Arabic word for tribe (*banu*, literally: the sons of) has for the most part been applied to al-Khidr in the Near East for centuries.

Herein it was also said concerning them, "The Khudr (of Banu) Muharib boasted of their black skin. The blacks are [indeed] called Khudr … by the Arabs." Moreover, according to Riley, author of the *Historical and Cultural Dictionary of Saudi Arabia*, "The higher incidence of Negroid phenotypic features appear in Tihama [Yemen], while the Bedouin, especially in the Nejd tends to the more classic 'Mediterranean' type, though there is Negroid admixture in some areas. In a large band from Khaibur and the Shammar area to the Wadi Dawasir there are extensive Bedouin-Negro mixes, the Banu Khudair" (Riley 1972; quoted in M'bantu & Muller 2013: 48).

These truths are extremely important as it was originally understood that the early Arabs were, in fact, predominantly Black. To prove this idea M'bantu and Muller said, "In the 9th century there was an Arabic writer named Uthman al-Jahiz who had an African grandfather. Al-Jahiz was one of the most educated men in the world of his day and was attached to the royal court of the Abbasid dynasty in Iraq. … Al-Jahiz also openly [talked] about how many Arab tribes have Black sections called *khudr*." He even declared of the Prophet's own grandfather, "The ten lordly sons of Abd al-Muttalib were very black in colour and large of body", and that the Abu Talib family, from whence the Prophet's cousin and son-in-law Ali came, "was more or less black-coloured."

Even so, it is acknowledged within Islam that the destiny of this Witness from the Banu al-Khidr is to bring and restore righteousness to the earth during the time of the great *eschaton*. He is, therefore, supposed to be the captain of the Messianic army to restore righteousness, and the witness of the Khidari tribe to remove wickedness. Moreover, it is also understood within Islam that he will be the main leader and rival standing against the Great *Dajjal*. At the same time, due to the corruption existing in the world during the days of *al-Dajjal*, it has also been understood that al-Khidr will face heavy opposition. However, this would not be before the *Dajjal* brings humanity to near ruin with his one-eyed mission to get revenge on humanity for his losses. Indeed, if we are perceptive we can see that actually he has in fact already done this. The world is currently, even right now, under the power of a villainous *Dajjal* (Imposter) and it will have to be one of al-Khidr that delivers us from the corruption he has brought to the world.

Still, when I use the word us in this statement, it is not to be taken as all-inclusive; the prophet Ezekiel wrote in his prophecies to the nations:

> *"The word of the Lord came again unto me, saying, Son of man, prophesy and say, Thus saith the Lord God; Howl ye, Woe worth the day! For the day is near, even the day of the Lord is near, a cloudly day; it shall be the time of the heathen. And the sword shall come upon Egypt, and great pain shall be in Ethiopia, when the slain shall fall in Egypt, and they shall take away her multitude, and her foundations shall be broken down. Ethiopia, and Libya, and Lydia, and all the mingled people, and Chub, and the men of the land that is in league, shall fall with them by the sword. Thus saith the Lord; They also that uphold Egypt shall fall; and the pride of her power shall come down: from the tower of Syene shall they fall in it by the sword, saith the Lord God. And they shall be desolate in the midst of the countries that are desolate, and her cities shall be in the midst of the cities that are wasted. And they shall know that I am the Lord, when I have set a fire in Egypt, and when all her helpers shall be destroyed. In that day shall messengers go forth from me in ships to make the careless Ethiopians afraid, and great pain shall come upon them, as in the day of Egypt for, lo, it cometh."*

To which the prophet Isaiah also continued, saying:

"In that day shall five cities in the land of Egypt speak the language of Canaan, and swear to the Lord of hosts; one shall be called, The city of destruction. In that day shall there be an altar to the Lord in the midst of the land of Egypt, and a pillar at the border thereof to the Lord. And it shall be for a sign and for a witness unto the Lord of host in the land of Egypt: for they shall cry unto the Lord because of the oppressors, and he shall send them a saviour, and a great one, and he shall deliver them. And the Lord shall be known to Egypt, and the Egyptians shall know the Lord in that day, and shall vow a vow unto the Lord, and perform it. And the Lord shall smite Egypt: he shall smite and heal it: and they shall return even to the Lord, and he shall be intreated of them, and shall heal them. In that day shall there be a highway out of Egypt to Assyria, and the Assyrian shall come into Egypt, and the Egyptian into Assyria, and the Egyptians shall serve with the Assyrians. In that day shall Israel be the third with Egypt and with Assyria, even a blessing in the midst of the land: Whom the Lord of host shall bless, saying, Blessed be Egypt my people, and Assyria the work of my hands, and Israel mine inheritance" (Ezekiel 30:1-9; Isaiah 19: 1-25).

At this point some Black people may argue that with the original Egyptians being Black, especially considering these Scriptures just quoted, why should we concern ourselves with the Hebrew God, Allah, and with his prophecies at all. The reason is that we are currently in, or are coming out of, the time of the heathen (or Gentiles) that the prophet Ezekiel spoke of. Even as Allah promised ships to take the Egyptians and Ethiopians captive, even so in our own history ships came to take us captive. Furthermore, as it may actually be even more important for us to recognise, the true and original Hebrew people were themselves most likely also Black people. In this, when al-Khidr comes, being fated to bring about the Divine Parousia, *he* will ultimately put an end to the time of the Gentile (this is also likely to be the reason why in Revelation the narrative of the two witnesses is presented right after an allusive reference to the time of the Gentiles).

This ending of the time of the Gentiles was perhaps given its most accurate description in the writing of the prophet Zephaniah when he wrote, "Therefore wait ye upon me, saith the Lord, until the day that I rise up to the prey: for my determination is to gather the nations, that I may assemble the kingdoms, to pour upon them mine indignation, even all my fierce anger: for all the earth shall be devoured with the fire of my jealousy. For then will I turn to the people a pure language, that they may all call upon the name of the Lord, to serve him with one consent. From beyond the rivers of Ethiopia my suppliants, even the daughter of my dispersed, shall bring mine offering. In that day shalt thou not be ashamed for all thy doings, wherein thou hast transgressed against me" (Zephaniah 3: 8-11).

Herein, those same Egyptians and Ethiopians that the prophet Ezekiel doomed into bondage during the time of the Gentiles, were in fact therefore of the Hebrew people dispersed into those lands, and were always destined towards that path. At the same time, those who they were fated to be in bondage to were always supposed to be of the Grecian people, and were also always destined towards their path. But as Allah would go on to say by his prophets Joel and Zechariah, "The children also of Judah and the children of Jerusalem have ye sold unto the Grecians, that ye might remove them far from their border." Therefore, "Turn you to the strong hold, ye prisoners of hope: even to day do I declare that I will render double unto thee; When I have bent Judah for me, filled the bow with Ephraim, and raised up thy sons, O Zion, against thy sons, O Greece, and made thee as the sword of a mighty man" (Joel 3: 6; Zechariah 9: 12, 13).

Consequently, it was further prophesied:

"Therefore behold, the days come, saith the Lord, that they shall no more say, The Lord liveth, which brought up the children of Israel out of the land of Egypt; But, The Lord liveth, which brought up and which led the seed of the house of Israel out of the north country, and from all countries whither I had driven them; and they shall dwell in their own land." For, "As I live, saith the Lord God, surely with a mighty hand, and with a stretched out arm, and with fury poured out, will I rule over you: And I will bring you out from the people, and will gather you out of the countries wherein ye are scattered, with a mighty hand, and with a stretched out arm, and with fury poured out. And I will bring you into the wilderness of the people, and there will I plead with you face to face. Like as I pleaded with your fathers in the wilderness of the land of Egypt, so will I plead with you, saith the Lord God" (Jeremiah 23: 7, 8; Ezekiel 20: 33-36).

Although it will all take place in a manner of, as noted by the apostle Paul, "every man in his own order: Christ the firstfruits; afterward they that are Christ's at his coming. Then cometh the end, when he shall have delivered up the kingdom to God, even the Father; when he shall have put down all rule and all authority and power. For he must reign, till he hath put all enemies under his feet." From all these images we get a clear idea of government, not by kingdom but by dictatorship, even as the classical Roman dictatorships were instituted by a general until order had been restored to the Roman provinces (of which all the apostles, including Paul and John, were observers); so it was acknowledged by their time that when the Messiah came he would have to seize and maintain power until every principality and power was crushed and order restored to the world. The idea of this seizing of power by Allah and his Messiah – with the Witness himself or herself probably being a chief captain – though foretold long before the first century, was never as graphically depicted except in the apostle John's Revelation.

Rosa Luxemburg also agreed that in a revolution the revolutionists "should and must at once undertake socialist measures in the most energetic, unyielding and unhesitant fashion, in other words, exercise a dictatorship, but a dictatorship of the *class*, not of a party or of a clique — dictatorship of the class, that means in the broadest public form on the basis of the most active, unlimited participation of the mass of the people". Conversely, whereas a modern economy — in the form of socialism or capitalism — sees dictatorship in the form of a class, a thearchic economy sees dictatorship in the form of the Messiah and his dominion of heaven: a dominion that is within us. Far from the dictatorship being that of a class over the rest of society, whether that class be a majority or a minority, the thearchy allows for self-government, trusting each to be ruled by the principles of justice and ethics as taught by the Messiah.

What makes the horseman of this white horse distinct from the other horsemen, however, is that he is given a crown and goes out to *nikao*, meaning to overcome, which happens to be the exact thing the Messiah encouraged the seven messianic communities to do in the opening cycle. Though there are many who consider this rider to be symbolic of 'Pestilence', there are no obvious clues to this in the actual description given of him *per se*. However, that is not to say there is absolutely no precedent for it. There is the possibility, due to his or her being destined to unleash plague and judgment upon the world, that this al-Khidr could very well be the embodiment and personification of Pestilence. Or some such theory could definitely be developed. While I cannot entirely deny these types of theories, it must still be appreciated that from the context of Revelation itself there is actually more proof of him or her being messianic than pestilent.

There are, however, some who would claim that the bow carried by this rider portends to something sinister. Yet most of these individuals somehow seem to have forgotten what David and Job said concerning Allah, "Yea, he sent out his arrows, and scattered them; and he shot out lightnings, and discomfited them." "For the arrows of the Almighty are within me, the poison whereof drinketh up my spirit: the terrors of God do set themselves in array against me." If even Allah has arrows and bow then it is quite fitting for his servants to also have such, even if only symbolically. In all this, what we can see here is that the first seal of the *Biblion* represented to the messianic communities of Asia Minor, both the first five trumpets and first five vials of the later chapters. The next five seals, however, were clearly supposed to represent for them the sixth trumpet and sixth vial. Finally, the seventh seal, trumpet, and vial were all most likely supposed to represent the same end: what we Muslims call the *Yaum al-Din* or Day of Judgment.

The Unstoppable Rise of an Insatiable Beast

From here we can see not so much an actual warring, but more so a brewing and preparing; the rising of a new form of government to take the place of all former ones. We also find a deeper meaning to Ezekiel's astral drama: "Therefore, son of man, prophecy and say unto Gog, Thus saith the Lord God; In that day when my people of Israel dwelleth safely, shalt thou not know it? And thou shalt come from thy place out of the north parts, thou, and many people with thee, all of them riding upon horses, a great company, and a mighty army: And thou shalt come up against my people of Israel, as a cloud to cover the land; it shall be in the latter days, and I will bring thee against my land, that the heathen may know me, when I shall be sanctified in thee, O Gog, before their eyes. Thus saith the Lord God; Art thou he of whom I have spoken in old time by my servants the prophets of Israel, which prophesied in those days many years that I would bring thee against them?"

Even so, as the Israel of the prophet Ezekiel's vision met with huge opposition upon their returning back from conflict, so the tide of conquest began to turn as the Lamb opened the second seal (6: 3, 4). At this point a fiery red horse and its horseman came to stand before the apostle John and the four living creatures. This horseman was at this time given the express authority and power to take peace from the earth and to start wars. He was also given a large sword with which to drive men to slay one another. The usual name given to this angel by those lay Bible traditionalists is therefore 'War,' as it has been believed that this angel represents the violent inclination within the souls of humanity.

But war has existed from time immemorial, and though modernity has brought with it more wars than at any other period of human history, this manifestation is more a result of ideological programming than of any violent instinct within people's souls. Even during the time of the classical empires and their religious vanities there were less wars than have happened since the arrival of modernity; and all the great killings that have occurred as a result of even the smaller of modern battles exceeds those of most of the larger wars of pre-modernity. In considering the reality of this situation we must come to understand that modernity has mainly brought with it the intensification of wars, which have effectively been much deeper than at previous historical epochs.

In our time, neo-colonialism and imperialist globalisation have taken on the semblance of respectability by modern definitions. As Western elites pursue ever wider capitalistic visions of expansion and development, countries such as the US and the countries within the EU and UK are currently in the process of repackaging the brand of imperialism, at least in the enterprise sense. However, Vladimir Lenin, in his own day, sought to unmask the brutality and chicanery of these kinds of endeavours, saying, "The building of railways seems to be a simple, natural, democratic, cultural and civilising enterprise … But as a matter of fact the capitalist threads, which in thousands of different intercrossings bind these enterprises with private property in the means of production in general, have converted this work of construction into an instrument for oppressing a thousand million people (in the colonies and semi-colonies), that is, more than half the population of the globe" (Lenin 2010: 5). Thus the enterprise and commercial empires of the great Western powers with their unrepentant mission to reconquer and carve up the world, have been emboldened to continue these enterprises ever since the rise of the first private companies of King James I's Great Britain in the early 1600s.

Still, as Lenin further pointed out, it is incalculably necessary to "understand the fundamental economic question, viz., the question of the economic essence of imperialism, for unless this is studied, it will be impossible to understand and appraise modern war and modern politics." True, modern imperialism may have come about as a result of European missionaries' desire to spread Victorian values and standards in the colonies, but it also created a desire within many of them to make settlements in those very colonies in the first place. Accordingly, as arch-colonialist Cecil Rhodes said to a friend of his in 1895 (just a few years before the Boer Wars),

> *"I was in the East End of London yesterday and attended a meeting of the unemployed. I listened to the wild speeches, which were just a cry for 'bread,' 'bread,' 'bread,' and on my way home I pondered over the scene and I became more than ever convinced of the importance of imperialism. … My cherished idea is a solution for the social problem, i.e., in order to save the 40,000,000 inhabitants of the United Kingdom from a bloody civil war, we colonial statesmen must acquire new lands [in other words, steal new lands] to settle the surplus population, to provide new markets for the goods produced by them in the factories and mines. The Empire, as I have always said, is a bread and butter question. If you want to avoid civil war, you must become imperialists."*

Obviously, we in our day, know the human cost of this vision Rhodes presented for the British working class; as Asante further explicated, "In the nineteenth century, Cecil John Rhodes sought to gain control of a large territory of southern Africa that was ruled by the Ndebele King Lobengula, and he sent emissaries to the powerful king in an effort to secure his consent. After many days of discussion with Lobengula, the white emissaries returned to Rhodes with the king's signature on a piece of paper. They told Rhodes that Lobengula had given him all of his territory, and Rhodes sent a column of soldiers into the area with the instruction to shoot any black on sight. Thus began the country of Rhodesia." Such an historically tragic occurrence gives a greater level of context as to the mind of Robert Mugabe, and his lack of trust or forgiveness for the White people of Zimbabwe (the decolonised name he gave to Rhodesia). When your people experience an historical tragedy like the murder of literally millions of their ancestors at the hands of a particular group, on the one hand, and you happen to lead a revolution against the descendants of that same group, on the other hand; surely you can be forgiven a level of hatred towards that said group, e.g. the Nazis – or was it the Palestinians(?).

Effectively, it is the spreading of propagations, and the narrations contained within those propagations, that allowed colonialism to also spread, as well as the ideas and values of colonialism. Modern colonialism thereby truly owes its development to the spreading of European propaganda. At the same time, it also owes a far larger amount of its progress to the development of capitalism. It further undeniably owes its continued maintenance to the naked brute force of aggressive militarism. Herein, as Fanon also said, "colonialism is not a thinking machine, nor a body endowed with reasoning faculties. It is violence in its natural state, and it will only yield when confronted with [an even] greater violence." Violence is how colonialism maintained itself, violence is how colonialism protected itself, and ultimately, violence brought colonialism to the brink of self-destruction; as Lenin would further explicate, "the war of 1914-18 was imperialistic (that is, an annexationist, predatory, plunderous war) on the part of both sides; it was a war for the division of the world, or the partition and repartition of colonies, 'spheres of influence' of finance capital, etc."

Thereby we can see that as the embodied development of finance capital – together with its active investment in the colonial project – continued it soon became clear, as Lenin further delineated, "Finance capital is not only interested in the already known sources of raw materials; it is also interested in potential sources of raw materials, because present-day technical development is extremely rapid, and because land which is useless today may be made fertile tomorrow if new methods are applied … and large amounts of capital are invested. This also applies to prospecting for materials, to new methods of working up and utilising raw materials, etc., etc. Hence, the inevitable striving of finance capital to extend its economic territory and even its territory in general."

This statement reveals to us the influence that finance, and hence economics, had on the spread and reproduction of imperialism. As the Western powers sought to compete with each other for geographical locations and geopolitical territories, the banking and manufacturing industries began to consolidate into financial trusts able to open up and invest in markets all over the world. For this cause, Lenin also mentioned, "It is beyond doubt … that capitalism's transition to the stage of monopoly capitalism, to finance capital, is *bound up* with the intensification of the struggle for the partition of the world." So, as what Lenin called, finance capital, began to consolidate, concentrating all wealth and resources into fewer and fewer hands, not only were they developing into monopoly industries, they were also exploiting and expanding into new global locations and territories.

In these situations, however, finance capital was more of an afterthought as most of the early and middle imperial powers of modern Europe already had a presence in the locations they were exploiting and sought later to influence. Nevertheless, the aftereffects of both the dislocation and relocation of the many resources (including the minerals, the wealth, and the human bodies and souls) of colonised territories – ultimately culminated in the abjectivity and impoverishment of those same colonised territories. Even Lenin was able to see how, "The growth of internal exchange, and particularly of international exchange, is [currently] the characteristic distinguishing feature of capitalism. The uneven and spasmodic character of the development of individual enterprises of individual branches of industry and individual countries, is [therefore] inevitable under the capitalist system." This insightful description and illustration of global conditions under the market tyranny of a capitalistic system allows us to appreciate that just as governments need checks and balances, so even the market needs checks and balances.

Concerning the further process of imperial development, Lenin went on to say, "When free competition in Great Britain was at its zenith, i.e., between 1840 and 1860, the leading British bourgeois politicians were opposed to colonial policy and were of the opinion that the liberation of the colonies and their complete separation from Britain was inevitable and desirable. … But [by] the end of the nineteenth century the heroes of the hour in England were Cecil Rhodes and Joseph Chamberlain, [both] open advocates of imperialism". Both these men would so outspokenly endorse the imperial project that, as leading socialist and editor, Chris Harman, later explained, "Those powers with empires sought to strengthen them by building up their military forces. Those without empires sought to take colonies and influence from those with. And, when it came to the crunch, they were prepared to wage world war against each other with Britain, France and Russia on the one side, and Germany and Austro-Hungary on the other."

That which would eventually lead up to World War I was originally conflicts and competitions over the carving up of the economic have-nots between the haves, and the political non-powers between the powers. Wars in 1898 between the US and Spain over Cuba and the Philippines. In 1899 between the British and the Boer settlers over southern Africa. In 1905 between Japan and Russia over Korea and northern China. In 1911 between Italy and Turkey over northern Africa (with a brief rivalry between France and Germany over Morocco in-between). And the war in 1912 between Russia and Austro-Hungary over the Balkans, which eventually led to World War I; were not national or even ideological wars as such, but were wars for ever broader economic and political spheres of influence.

With the global expansion of economic empires, arose the need to strengthen the military presence in such global territories so as to deter any abuses or mishandling of finances by said occupied territory or the capturing and annexing of the occupied territory by a rival empire. Economic-colonisation thereby led to military-colonisation; and after the missionary gains of the Victorian era also added to the mix the end result was inevitably settler- and spatial-colonisation. Fanon also confirmed this reality, stating, "The colonial world is a Manichaean world. It is not enough for the settler to delimit physically, that is to say with the help of the army and the police force, the place of the native. As if to show the totalitarian character of colonial exploitation the settler [also] paints the native as a sort of quintessence of evil" (Fanon 1969: 32).

Though it could be said that this process of demonising the other began from the time of slavery, the process was improved, refined, modified, intensified, and even pathologised, during colonialism. Indeed, colonialism's brutality towards the native fed inexorably into the West's racist sentiments and ideas about the natives. "Racism stares one in the face for it so happens that it belongs in a characteristic whole: that of the shameless exploitation of one group of men by another which has reached a higher stage of technical development. This is why military and economic oppression generally precedes, makes possible, and legitimatizes racism." Basically, as Victorian morality and capitalist competition took Europeans to the lands of Africa, Asia, Australia, and the Americas to expand, exploit, and extract wealth, their interactions eventually led to colonial racism.

At the same time, we can also appreciate how both of the economic systems of modernity, capitalism and socialism, effectively came to crushed out all moral, economic, and military opposition within the territories thus conquered by colonialism. Thereby they appreciably made all past economic systems of those territories either *invisiblised* or appear obsolete. Kwame Nkrumah especially noted this reality in reference to pre-modern Africa, noting, "Under communalism ... all land and means of production belonged to the community. When a certain piece of land was allocated to an individual for his personal use, he was not free to do as he liked with it since it still belonged to the community. Chiefs were strictly controlled by counsellors and were removable." The majority of Africans lived under this type of economic system for centuries (including King Lobengula), but it was unfortunately incapable of withstanding the enormous pressures of modernisation bought to bear by colonial violence.

Nkrumah said concerning Africa's historical progression towards the modernity forced upon it by colonialism, "Subsistence agriculture was gradually destroyed and Africans were compelled to sell their labour power to the colonialist, who turned their profits into capital". "With the growth of commodity production, mainly for export, single crop economies developed completely dependent on foreign capital. The colony became a sphere for investment and exploitation."

What we observe from here is that as modernity was imported into Africa from the West it substantially affected the continent causing it to not only surrender its raw materials, minerals, and Black bodies, minds, and souls to colonial powers but to be completely dependent on foreign capital for survival. Thereby Western capital became dominant in Africa through colonialism, and industrial development, along with railways, ports, engineering, construction, and, most importantly, fictitious capital, all these becoming dominant concerns for Africa.

Indeed, continents like Africa went through a rapid modernisation during colonialism that created the need for greater foreign investment and more foreign capital where it could be said that none formerly existed. Nkrumah further delineated on the subject: "the spread of private enterprise, together with the needs of the colonial administrative apparatus, resulted in the emergence of first a petty bourgeois class and then an urban bourgeois class of bureaucrats, reactionary intellectuals, traders, and others, who became increasingly part and parcel of the colonial economic and social structure" (Nkrumah 2006: 15). Yet investment in Africa would still continue, even after colonialism fell, as several countries sought partial import substitution.

An example of this is in that all of French Africa chose to come under the franc. Moreover, all "their currencies have been stabilized on a fixed parity with the French franc and have a total guarantee from the French Treasury. These States pay their receipts of French francs into operation accounts in the French Treasury. These accounts can be overdrawn and the States can draw on them against their own currencies to an unlimited extent. Obviously, however, whatever the theoretical-position, the international financial position of these countries is subject to control in that at any time their operation accounts in the French Treasury could be blocked, as was done in the case of Guinea" (Nkrumah 2022: 24).

Yet, all this took place before the US Treasury became dominant in Africa. Here, Nkrumah added that there was, even in his time, "increasing American investments in the continent's extractive industries and the growth of United States participation in financial establishments on this continent. American banking houses are making inroads into territories formerly catered for solely by European and British banks. The French banks still dominate in the former French countries and the Belgians in the Congo; but this is frequently a front for American participation." Interestingly enough, a new phenomenon was beginning to occur around about this time as the ex-colonies were going through the process of decolonisation.

Nkrumah called this new phenomenon neo-colonisation, explaining that the "neo-colonialism of today represents imperialism in its final and perhaps its most dangerous stage … In place of colonialism as the main instrument of imperialism we have today neo-colonialism" (Nkrumah 2022: 1). In this current system the only neo-colonial power left in the world, and the one that is presently consuming most of the planet, is the Great United States Empire (GUSE). Nkrumah thereby continued, showing in particular that America's foreign investments in Africa before World War II were only 3 percent, and that less than 5 percent of Africa's trade was with the US. But by the fall of 1949 certain British and American bankers colluded to establish American investments in the continent and other parts of the British Empire. He further affirmed that two months later, meetings were established in Africa between American and French bankers with a similar purpose in mind.

Ultimately, as Nkrumah made perfectly clear, "The essence of neo-colonialism is that the State which is Subject to it is, in theory, independent and has all the outward trappings of international sovereignty. In reality its economic system and thus its political policy is directed from outside." It is for this reason, he went on to say, "the African bourgeoisie, the class which thrived under colonialism, is the same class … benefiting under the post-independence, neocolonial period." Hereby, even though Africa undeniably has conditions of abject poverty within it, urban Africa currently experiences what Engberg-Pedersen et al. called conjunctural poverty.

Within this situation, the formal sector, paid employment, and real wage decreases have been the major obstacle. At the same time, rural Africa experiences a huge differentiation with poverty being far more absolute. Here, poverty is measured in indicators such as: "food insecurity and malnutrition, lack of proper shelter, physical isolation in inaccessible rural areas, and vulnerability to external shocks, diseases etc. … The rural/urban gap is also significant in regard to access to safe water, education and health services." This rural/urban gap could be considered a form of class warfare in practice between the majority African peasantry and the minority African bourgeoisie.

Within this particular class warfare, this biopolitical warfare, fighting mainly takes place in the subjectivities of the African people based on the idea that Africa is nothing more than these uninhabitable locations of immense and abject poverty. Essentially, biopolitics itself is when politics is used to control and discipline minds and bodies: when life becomes political and when the political, economic, and cultural "overlap" into everyday life. US capital has itself become biopolitical through the multimedia, multiculture, multi-religion, and politics itself, all becoming commodified and commercialised. The biopolitical nature of the GUSE thus causes those countries that rebel against the dollar to be drawn into a problematic situation. With the United States currently being the world banker, to need money at all places a country at a disadvantage to America. Thus American capital is not only biopolitical it is also globalised.

This was that "New World Order" spoken of by Bush Sr. at the end of the Cold War. War machines like NATO, though no longer necessary, were not abandoned, in actual fact, they were enlarged. The US after the ending of the Cold War actually spent more on arms and nuclear weapons up to September 11, 2001. Then with the incoming of 9/11 and the "War on Islam," they went on to spend a total of $379 billion in their military budget. And so the GUSE has become the current imperial power of the world. Going further still we can see one very obvious truth: the earnest manifestation of prophecy is not by the hand of humanity, nor will it be the duty of humanity to fulfil, it is only by the hand of Allah. Again, the many small battles, wars, and conflicts of global history have really just been preparation for Allah's big showdown. Lately, as we all can now see, there has been emerging one monopolistic superpower over all of global politics.

The Empire that Debt Built

At the opening of the next seal (6: 5, 6) there came to stand before the apostle John and the four living creatures a black horse and its horseman. This horseman himself carried a pair of scales in his hand, and there came a voice from the midst of the four living creatures that gave the impression of a scarcity of food and of near famine conditions. For this cause, this horseman is usually called by those who know of his existence, 'Famine.' This truth is a reality that is given an even broader explication in the prophet Ezekiel's astral vision, "Thus saith the Lord God; It shall also come to pass, that at the same time shall things come into thy mind, and thou shalt think an evil thought: And thou shalt say, I will go up to the land of unwalled villages; I will go to them that are at rest, that dwell safely, all of them dwelling without walls, and having neither bars nor gates, To take a spoil, and to take a prey; to turn thine hand upon the desolate places that are now inhabited, and upon the people that are gathered out of the nations, which have gotten cattle and goods, that dwell in the midst of the land."

Now by all modern economic interpretations a famine is a time of economic downturn when the demand for food is greater than the supply. However, such a phenomenon could never really happen in our times. What can happen is that the food that is available is too expensive for the poverty stricken inhabitants of a country to afford (in which case most of the food gets dumped out and wasted – or they may be given away to foodbanks as a corporation tax write-off); but ultimately there is food enough to feed the populations of the entire planet easily. So where is the problem then? There is not *money* enough in any particular country to feed its own inhabitants easily – and that is with both consumer shopping and state sponsorship in place. However the economic system of the apostle John's time looked there is one thing that is definitely undeniable, as a slavery- and market-based system it obviously had its own fluctuations and downturns. From this we can see that famine conditions themselves come about due to the fact that the purpose of food within every market economy is primarily to make a profit and not to feed or help the hungry.

Accordingly, modernity has seen various moments of economic downturns so great that it has called them Great Depressions or Great Recessions. In these times famine conditions affected not only a country but the entire planet. That is because the modern system has integrated all monies into a universal market system. Yet, as we just said, every market system, from their first formation in the ancient states of Africa and Asia, all go through their own cycles of famine and plenty. Then added to that is the fact that integrated money-capital, far from saving the system from the brunt of difficulty, only exacerbates the difficulty through what socialists have dubbed *the falling rate of profits*. Simply put, the increasing wealth of the few super-rich bourgeoisies inevitably takes money from the moderately rich or not as rich bourgeoisies. In sum, all monies are getting concentrated into the hands of fewer and fewer people, while those who were rich today become moderately affluent tomorrow, and those who were moderately affluent today become poor tomorrow, etc.

To go with this the devaluation of money through inflation and interest rates has meant that money by today's standards can do far less than money by the standards of five years ago, let alone ten or twenty years ago. Again, this is due to the rising of the profits and capital gains of the very few super-rich, which must be compensated for by taking profits and monies from the not as rich. These stolen funds, though increasing the wealth of the super-rich bourgeois individual, cause the average rate of profits for the *class* of the bourgeoisie to steadily decrease. In order to make up for this difficulty the national system of the country is forced to print more money to curve out this discrepancy. This solution may dupe the people, it may even dupe the struggling bourgeoisie, but it cannot dupe the system, which to balance out the losses devalues the excess money-capital produced. This devaluation of national currency in turn leads to rising prices, which is the by-product of inflation, which itself precedes recession.

To solve this problem of the falling rate of profits companies have done one or two of three things: (i) expand the market overseas, (ii) lengthen the hours of exploitation, or (iii) get more out of the workers in the time they have through improved technology. Lately, employers have been doing the third but as they have not confronted the central issue of market mechanisms the overall rate of profits for individual capitalists continues decreasing. Further, as competition between various Western powers also increases and the rush to open up new markets for the purpose of strengthening global hegemony grows, an obviously very familiar idea within the mechanisms of the system has ultimately been regaining legitimacy: imperialism.

In the 1870s and 1880s this situation existed with the great European powers, driving each to expand their individual spheres of influence; and thus causing overseas investment to rise substantially with land, labour, and other raw materials being cheap there and capital being scarce there. These opportunities to attain cheap resources (like diamonds and gold from Africa's vast quantity of diamond- and goldmines), plus the added opportunity to export their commercial products to the now opened up markets of their colonies, would all further allow the European powers to become fabulously wealthy. Effectively, by stealing wealth and prosperity from the colonies of Africa, Asia, Latin America, and Australia, Europe was able to make herself and her individual countries into the dominant powers of the world.

"Obviously, out of [their] enormous *super-profits* (since they [were] obtained over and above the profits which capitalists squeeze out of the workers of their 'home' country) it [was also] quite *possible to bribe* the labour leaders and the upper stratum of the labour aristocracy" (Lenin 2010: 9). Essentially, these corrupted European labour leaders soon became far more interested and concerned with maintaining the global legitimation and superordination of imperialism than with concretising or reproducing any just or ethical society – and this phenomenon was not unique to Europeans. As Fanon noted, "Colonialism hardly ever exploits the whole of a country. It contents itself with bringing to light the natural resources, which it extracts, and exports to meet the needs of the mother country's industries, thereby allowing certain sectors of the colony to [also] become relatively rich."

This issue is therefore one of extreme delicacy, as most people in this Western world system will be, and have been, willing to fight and die in order to preserve the system as it is, failing to appreciate that the system itself is a ticking time bomb of economic chaos and degeneration. Unfortunately, neither those relatively rich nor their relatively poor subordinates have been willing to question, challenge, or problematise, let alone counter, the Western compensation system; fearing that the loss of the market would mean the overall loss of incentive, and thus the social deviation and economic impoverishment of society. At the same time, they almost fanatically believe that the maintenance and reproduction of the system means the overall concretisation of prosperity. What they fail to appreciate is that the maintenance and reproduction of the system will concretise nothing but mass disorder and mass impoverishment on an ever grander scale.

The social aetiology of the GUSE's current neo-colonial expansion of market economics started from around the mid- to late-twentieth century. Prior to that, to all intents and purposes, Britain was the leading and largest empire of the world, taking the position of world manufacturer, world banker, and world marketer for the purpose of the maintenance and stability of the international dominance of British industry. The Sterling Area was thus the international storehouse of finance capital. Indeed, industrial-colonialism was purely a result of the collusion of finance capital and monopoly capital. Britain also established the "sanctity of debt" ideology within its debtor nations (the colonies) in order to keep them subservient and dependent.

In those days, the United States was a big banker but not "the World Banker." Moreover, the United States had no interest in becoming a world power, but mainly to stick to its own isolationist plan in economics, politics, and geopolitics. Things, however, would change after World War I as the world sank into an economic Depression. The US, at that time, began to build up its stock of gold reserves obsessively. By the end of World War II, the US was in control of almost 60 percent of the world's gold supply. This gave the US a very powerful and effective bargaining chip as, "Apart from metallic coinage, domestic currency is a form of debt, but one that nobody really expects to be [paid; as the futile attempting] by governments to repay their debts beyond a point would extinguish their [own national] monetary base" (Hudson 2021: 16).

Hereby, at the end of World War II, Europe, which was the chief colonising agent of the world, would also become the chief debtor to the United States in the world. America, at that time, had investments in banks all over Germany, Italy, France,

Belgium, Great Britain, etc. Thus, the US would enter the world stage and would enter it with force. Using its dominant position, as possessing the world's largest gold supply, it convinced Britain, and through Britain the rest of Europe, as well as the entire Sterling Area, to use the International Monetary Fund to stabilise each of their own currencies by the gold standard. Essentially, all currencies in the Sterling Area and Franc Area were, as a result, to measure their value at $35 an ounce of gold. Thereby, "foreign exchange rates were [effectively] linked to the dollar, which became the world's key currency, accepted in international reserves and used to pay foreign debts in lieu of gold."

On top of all that, the World Bank was also established in the United States, despite British protests that it be established in Europe (and, for the purpose of showing all cards on the table, it was established in Washington DC, as – according to their top officials – the Bank and Fund should never finance policies the United States believed went against their national interests). Indeed, the National Advisory Council on International Monetary and Financial Policies (NAC) was set up by the US government to oversee the Bank, the Fund, and all other inter-governmental lending institutions. According to Hudson, "The U.S. executive directors of the Bank and Fund were responsible directly to the NAC for their votes in these organizations."

As a result of all this manoeuvring, the system was able to sustain a somewhat stable economic growth period from the 1940s to the 1970s. Basically, before the 1970s all Western monies became measurable economic units. The system only began to fall apart in the 1970s when Richard Nixon took all the countries then in – what was by that time called – the dollar area off the gold standard. As money was needed to fund the Vietnam War, and as the workers and unions started getting greedy for revolution without actually being prepared to fight an actual revolution, or even knowing what they were fighting for, the economic system effectively took a downturn. That revolutionary spirit, which was a remnant of the 1960s, eventually turned to clouds of hostility and disillusionment as the world did not change nor become a better place. To make up for the discrepancy the people began to march and demonstrate, but not to actually fight. Thus the cities of the West ground to a halt, but with nobody seizing power crisis was inevitable.

Furthermore, with the diabolical development of fiat currency by the changes instituted by the Nixon administration, the dependent, and thus valueless, nature of global currency was thereby officially exposed to the world. Today all monies are merely numbers on a screen, bank notes and statements, or pieces of paper with fancy stuff in and on them. Money no longer exists in a substantial sense, hence why crypto was able to disrupt the banking system so easily. The truth is, at this time, all currency is merely an IOU from a country's own central bank agreeing that the value of that piece of paper will be paid by the government if it should fail. This system becomes even more diabolical when we remember that all central banks themselves have no real power to determine the value of their own currency as, since the creation of the Bank and the Fund, all currencies in the dollar area are valued only through the dollar.

What all this therefore produces is a system whereby the stability and strength of all currencies within the dollar area (which by now is *virtually* the entire globe) are guaranteed merely by the strength of the US dollar. Nevertheless, the US dollar, like all other currencies since 1971, has no value or strength of its own, all it is is paper with fancy shit in and on it. Ultimately, the US dollar is, and thereby all currencies within the dollar area are, basically guaranteed by an American IOU, i.e. debt, or better yet, a promise to pay us back. But again, with what? Currency(!) In other words, all the banks of the world, and all the currencies of the world, are held together by nothing more than numbers on a screen and pieces of paper with some shit in and on them. Worse still, this is not the only form of fictitious capital that exists within the current economic system: all stocks, shares, assets, bonds, options, equity, debt, credit, interest, and even wages, are themselves only forms of fictitious capital.

Imagine for a moment a wannabe investor going to a bank and depositing $5,000 cash. Apparently, for every dollar deposited the bank is to receive from their central bank, and thereby from a US promise, an additional interest based on their country's nationally agreed upon interest rate (all really just numbers on a group of screens). Then, now, the investor desires to purchase $20,000 worth of shares in a company, to get this she goes to the same bank and takes out a loan (just numbers in a bank account, and a piece of paper with both records and the bank's logo on it) for $20,000. Then she receives the loan and uses it to purchase the shares (which in turn are only just pieces of paper with a company's logo and a country's seal on them, and words and numbers on a digital screen). In time the company may go public so the shares become stocks or securities (both fictitious names to denote a change when nothing has really changed but words and numbers on several different screens).

Overall, all that really changes monetary-wise is the value *society* now gives to numbers as they become larger or enter into different word groupings and categories on those screens spoken of here so cynically. In other words, the entire edifice of finance capitalism is currently based on nothing more than numbers on screens. Herein also lies the central danger of finance capitalism, it deifies these numbers on screens giving them greater value than the lives, pains, and struggles of living, feeling beings, human and otherwise. Indeed, it even reduces living beings themselves to nothing more than numbers on a screen to be graphed and charted for the purpose of nothing more than to extract profits from them.

Reductions like this cause reactions from economists when chasms like economic crises occur, to consider such events nothing more than the system merely clearing the way to allow better businesses to consume smaller, less successful ones. Or to expand overseas or globally into new territory to disrupt the businesses of the local population of those territories. The acquired smaller businesses will either have to accept being consumed to save their lives or go completely bust during an economic downturn; while the survival of any indigenous people and their communal businesses become more and more tenuous due to the arrival of bigger Western businesses and cheaper Western products. Among the struggling workers in both cases, however, we find nothing but layoffs, wage decreases, or job depreciations all around.

All this inevitably leads to the concentration of wealth – again, just numbers on a screen and based entirely on an empty and unfulfillable promise – into fewer and fewer hands and thus to monopoly capital; and transnational monopoly capital is really just another form of imperial capital, as these corporate empires grow to take over the game even with their currencies of wind. Again, as capitalism gives way to corporate imperialism jobs and wages are not only at stake but are unsaveable. So, like it or not, the workers of today will be the underclass of tomorrow, even as the intellectuals of today, though usually unsuited to self-employment, in order to make ends-meet, will either have to take such or suffer complete joblessness.

This is all due to the process of what economists call *the business cycle of bust and boom*, or famine and plenty. To give the standard economist explanation of this process and why they say we go through it at all, to those who may have never heard of it; I shall now take you through *their* version of what it is. To start with booms are when businesses are doing well; profits are good; prices are reasonably set; wages are decent; companies are able to expand, make more branches, and invest in more productive property. With more companies expanding raw materials get scarce and their prices go up, which eventually leads to prices going up all around, thus to inflation. Inflation soon leads to bust or "recession", where unemployment rises along with bankruptcy; companies close down the new branches, lose millions, or get bought-out by larger companies.

Life in these times is pretty much miserable for everybody, and they seem to be unbeatable, but eventually there will come a time when smaller businesses will feel comfortable investing again and soon they will grow, and as they grow other companies will grow through them. A furniture store is doing well enough so they invest in more furniture. This gives work to more carpenters, who in turn give more work to loggers, who in turn give more work to truck manufacturers, who in turn help the steel and tire industries, who help other industries grow and eventually the whole system begins to grow again leading to another boom. So the *business cycle* is bust-boom-bust-boom.

This is the standard economist interpretation, however, another explanation for economic crises, and thereby famine, is that the current market system based on supply and demand seems overall to prioritise demand. That means, if the people/market (or *your* people/market) are not demanding or desiring your product, service, brand, or business, it will disappear in this Darwinian world of commerce. This market system therefore, of necessity, requires marketing and skills in marketing otherwise, again, instant death by irrelevance. This sort of system can and does work in the short term. However, in the long run, some companies, in order to stay relevant, popular, or even alive, will hawk to the public certain goods, services, and information that does nothing for them and only saves or fattens the pockets of the marketers and the businesses they are working for.

Unless we can create a co-ordinated operation to provide for the people, not what they currently demand, but more so what they genuinely need. One that, at the same time, also allows them the option of wider choices through a non-intrusive, non-bureaucratic, yet decentralised participatory methodology: one such as the programme I have outlined within my own conception of Black syndicalism (Islam 2024). Whatever programme is put in place will either limit the freedom of choice of the individual, in which case oppression, or limit the capacities of the system, in which case chaos. The two must work together, that is, limited market *and* limited state. To take power from the one without, at the same time, taking power from the other leaves an imbalance and inequality in the societal superstructure where power resides either in wealth or force.

Nevertheless, for the lack of this form of societal superstructure, and due to the inefficiency of the modern free market system, economists have been forced to resort to the now obsolete, now reviving, methods of their forebears, thus giving rise to neo-colonialism. From here the current and continuing war crises will remain the inevitable and persistent outcome. Moreover, we can now perceive that the imperialistic wars of 1914-18 and 1939-45 were merely a prelude of good things to come if we do not start looking harder for better solutions. The current global expansion of corporate enterprises are reminiscent of those of the late nineteenth and early twentieth centuries before the outbreak of global war. Here again, the stage appears to be being set for a very dramatic and climactic conclusion.

The Power of Absolute Power

With the opening of the fourth seal (6: 7, 8) the apostle John saw standing before him a pale horse whose horseman was called "Death," and Hades followed with him, probably riding on his own pale horse. Death was then given power over the fourth part of the earth, to kill by sword, famine, plague, and the wild beasts of the earth; and having a partner like Hades by his side he was completely prepared for what was about to take place. The mission set before him he had had in mind from the very beginning; he had been watching and waiting for the onslaught he would be sent out to inflict from his very creation. The pursuit of his vision and his destiny was declared all the more forcefully as the prophet Ezekiel's drama continued, "Therefore, thou son of man, prophesy against Gog, and say, Thus saith the Lord God; Behold, I am against thee, O Gog, the chief prince of Meshech and Tubal: And I will turn thee back, and leave but the sixth part of thee, and will cause thee to come up from the north parts, and will bring thee upon the mountain of Israel: And I will cause thine arrows to fall out of thy right hand."

While Death and Hades have definitely interfered in human lives, caused great and tragic loss, and brought with them an overabundance of suffering, this has all been within the remit of their sovereignty. Indeed, as Achille Mbembe also pointed out, "The ultimate expression of sovereignty largely resides in the power and capacity to dictate who is able to live and who must die." Herein Foucault's biopolitics becomes the defining of who gets to live and how they are to live, the defining of livelihoods and lifestyles. But as every light casts a shadow, so the shadow of biopolitics is Mbembe's necropolitics: the defining of who must die, how they are to die, and for what reason they must die.

In defining who dies and for what reason they must die, Death and Hades do not necessarily use only violence, or what could be called "hard power," to achieve this goal and objective. We have seen how the imperial forces of Europe eventually exploded into global war due to the expansive nature of capitalism. We have also seen how finance capital can turn into monopoly capital, and thus into imperial capital, simply by the investment into international projects ultimately leading to the extraction of resources from a colony in order to benefit a "mother country," whichever European country that happened to be. While the first, and the defining of who must die, may technically be seen as clear expressions of hard power, the second, and the defining of a reason for which they must die, could themselves be considered expressions of what is called in the political sphere "soft power."

In his book on the subject, Joseph Nye presented an effective definition of what he believed soft power to be, "It is the ability to get what you want through attraction rather than coercion or payments. It arises from the attractiveness of a country's culture, political ideals, and policies." Hereby, we can see that though Death and Hades definitely use coercion and aggressiveness to accomplish their tasks on one level, it is also clear that that is not the only means they use. They are very capable of also using seduction and attractiveness to accomplish their goals. Herein lies the genius of Allah, through his own use of soft power, he has been able to make their goals – those of Death and Hades – actually be the very goals and intentions he has always had for them, and even for the world.

Conversely, the hard power of Death and Hades has been explored by many authors, movies, and narratives throughout history. What I, however, intend to do is explain a little deeper how their soft power can be used effectively, and even devastatingly, to cause not only mass murder and death, but even the potential genocide of an entire race right under the noses of the international community. First, we have already seen how soft power is generally used by governments, cultures, and groupings to basically seduce, or at least inspire, others into following a path. Nye said again, "Seduction is always more effective than coercion, and many values like democracy, human rights, and individual opportunities are deeply seductive. As General Wesley Clark put it, soft power 'gave us an influence far beyond the hard edge of traditional balance-of-power politics.' But attraction can turn to repulsion if we act in an arrogant manner and destroy the real message of our deeper values."

Clearly, the idea that Death and Hades can or would use something so undervalued and underappreciated as soft power (even the name itself has an air of weakness about it) may leave something of a fowl taste in many of our mouths. Nevertheless, if we explore the tragic conflict between the Hutu and the Tutsi we will be able to see how soft power and representation could be used to create, both an aggressive genocidal attack, and an equally aggressive genocidal response, all while the international community looks on assuming both to simply be a case of rivalrous or tribal (that is, cultural/ideological) conflicts. Thereby outright genocidal activities can be masked through manipulating the public into sympathising with and toleration of those who perpetrate such genocidal activities.

Keen (2012) spoke on the usage of what he called the dangerous template of "ethnic war," and how it potentially blinds global populations as to the true, or at least desired, intentions of certain regimes. In this case, he spoke on, "A tragic example [being] Rwanda in 1994. Here, the world's media (and indeed the UN secretary-general) tended to present mass violence as a spontaneous 'Hutu versus Tutsi' conflict that was driven by senseless hatred – a damaging misrepresentation that helped to delay international recognition that this was actually a carefully planned genocide. In the crucial first four weeks of the Rwandan genocide, both the UN Security Council and the UN Secretariat focused their attention on the 'civil war' in Rwanda, virtually ignoring the genocide and the possibility of organising peacekeepers to prevent or reduce it."

In this particular instant, soft power – presenting the war as nothing more than a civil conflict or tribal war – blinded the masses as to what was really going on. The Tutsi were being systematically and purposively targeted for extermination and annihilation at the hands of various Hutu groupings so as to completely remove them from the Rwandan territory. The Hutu basically saw the Tutsi ethno-tribal grouping as only a hindrance to their own progression and mobility. Herein immigration and ethnocentric rhetoric were writ-large allowing xenophobic ambitions to cloud judgments on a tribal level. On the political and diplomatic level, however, ignorance and inability were being claimed by all governmental factions, in response to the various attacks being perpetrated against the Tutsi.

All realities very similar in our own time to that occurring in the current Israel/Palestine conflict. Governments can use their soft power to claim ignorance and impotence concerning the threat of an all-powerful monster beyond their control or can use it to hide the grand atrocities they themselves have been committing, without end, against their opponent. Effectively, throwing off or passing off as "innocent ethnic rivalries" any genocidal activities they themselves have been committing. Either way, soft power is being used to present something to the public; and either way, what is being presented to the public is a lie. Public presentation and representation are key assets of soft power, and both can be used to deadly effect. Here, Israeli historian Benny Morris painted a clear picture, explaining the tragic circumstances under which the Zionist forces invaded and seized Palestine in 1948. He explained, there was a much larger amount and extent of massacres than he expected, as well as far more cases of rape – many of which ending in murder – than he originally presumed.

Morris, himself an ardent and loyal Zionist, even to the point of excusing these horrors, when confronted on the idea that what really happened in 1948 was a Zionist attempt at systematic ethnic cleansing, said in their defence, "There are circumstances in history that justify ethnic cleansing. I know that this term is completely negative in the discourse of the twenty-first century, but when the choice is between ethnic cleansing and genocide – the annihilation of your people – I prefer ethnic cleansing." While such a logic – and I speak here with the deepest sarcasm – may have been excusable in the immediate aftermath of the Holocaust, the Palestinians were neither the perpetrators of the Holocaust nor did they have any connection to any of the sufferings Jewish people up to that point had ever endured. Moreover, if we look at the current *literal genocide* being perpetrated *by them* against the Palestinians, and the understanding that the Palestinians never had any intention of ever committing genocide against the Israelis, in spite of what had been, and even today still is, going on there, makes the whole Israeli cause in the current war somewhat laughable if it were not so tragic.

Instead, the Palestinians are painted as some horrific, villainous, and almost undefeatable monster that has it out for all the Jews in both "Israel" and the world over. Such rhetoric then couples with the showing of very strategic images, and the telling of very strategic stories, concerning only certain goings on in the actual war. Many times, they even mistranslate the Arabic or Israeli language to the public with no other intent but to spread the narrative that they want the West to hear. This is irresponsible journalism by, in many cases, non-journalists having no obligation to the journalist code of ethics, using Israel's soft power and global support to literally, not rhetorically – as is the case with their Muslim neighbours – wipe out an entire ethnic grouping.

Essentially, these types of individuals claim Islam has an historic hostility towards the Jews (usually Ashkenazi), as though we Muslims, Semites ourselves, are anti-Semitic, having anti-Semitism somehow built into the very fabric of our religion and traditions. But what does the Quran, the most authoritative book in the Islamic tradition, and the basis for all Islamic laws and principles, actually say concerning the Jews?

> *And certainly Allah made a covenant with the Children of Israel, and We raised up among them twelve chieftains. And Allah said: Surely I am with you. If you keep up prayer and pay the poor-rate and believe in My messengers and assist them and offer to Allah a goodly gift, I will certainly cover your evil deeds, and cause you to enter Gardens wherein rivers flow. But whoever among you disbelieves after that, he indeed strays from the right way. But on account of their breaking their covenant We cursed them and hardened their hearts. They alter the words from their places and neglect a portion of that whereof they were reminded. And thou wilt always discover treachery in them excepting a few of them – so pardon them and forgive. Surely Allah loves those who do good (to others).*

Firstly, take note that in Islam Allah is not impartial. He only loves those who do good. This idea is fundamentally different from the Western tradition that teaches the idea and concept of an unconditionally impartial God. Such a God, however, would thereby ignore corruption, deceit, injustice, and oppression. It is almost like, of course White people would promote such a God, they are currently in their position of power knowing that they only gained that power either through their own corruption and exploitation, or through the corruption and exploitation their ancestors inflicted on people of colour (POCs) around the world. What the Quran, and the God of the Quran, were saying here was that Allah has a preferential option – not for the poor, or for the majority, or for the oppressed, or for the victimised, or for the racialised, or for the gendered, or for even the religious, all representing groupings that could just as easily become unjust and corrupted if given the right opportunity – only for those who do good.

Secondly, and I want to make this very clear, this Scripture is a far cry from "an historic hostility towards the Jews." I must also here fervently remind you that when the Prophet here used the words, "Children of Israel" he was speaking specifically of a Falashic group, not the Ashkenazic, who at that time had not yet converted to Judaism. This Falashic group would have thereby been an authentic Black Hebrew grouping to match the time and location that all this took place in.

So then, what about the conclusion that Islam was spread "by the edge of the sword," i.e., that it is a religion of conquest and only by reason of conquest was ever accepted? Well, let us here return to the Quran to see the actual words the Prophet spoke concerning those who were, not only non-practitioners of Islam, but, themselves practitioners of the very pagan/polytheist religion Islam sought to replace: "And thus their associate-gods have made fair-seeming to many polytheists the killing of their children, that they may cause them to perish and obscure for them their religion. And if Allah had pleased, they would not have done it, so leave them alone with that which they forge" (Quran 6: 137).

Again, this is a far cry from the biblical tradition, particularly the Old Testament, which if misread or misinterpreted could just as easily be used to promote and justify *literal* genocidal practices, such as where it is written, "Thus saith the Lord of hosts, I remember that which Amalek did to Israel, how he laid wait for him in the way, when he came up from Egypt. Now go and smite Amalek, and utterly destroy all that they have, and spare them not; but slay both men and women, infant and suckling, ox and sheep, camel and ass" (1Samuel 15: 2, 3). And just in case there is any further doubt about it, the prophet Samuel cursed the Kish Dynasty of Saul because of King Saul's failure to actually go through with the complete and total genocide of the people of Amalek.

Indeed, this kind of mentality is very similar to that of those who attempted to inflict the Rwandan genocide. Herein, in order to get the full story of this situation we may have to start at the very beginning, in the aftermath of World War I. According to researcher and social media influencer, Lynae Vanee, after the Allied victory in World War I, the League of Nations gave possession of all German colonies in Africa, that is, of Rwanda and Burundi, to Belgium. On top of Belgium's already possessing the so-called Congo Free State, the new colonies now expanded their African colonial territory to three places. But Belgian rule, for the most part, was mainly through corporations, so as to extract Africa's many resources, and through missionary work. Add to this cocktail the popularity the Europe of the time of the doctrine of Eugenics, and particularly of Belgian Eugenics – a field that was built around a concept called anthropometry: in which a person's or racial group's capacity to learn and develop in science, ethics, rhetorics, aesthetics, hygienics, and advanced civilisation was determined by their bodily type, shape, and measurements.

Ultimately, what ended up happening was, using Belgian Eugenics, many of the Belgian authorities of Belgian East Africa assumed the Tutsi tribe were racially and biologically superior to the Hutu tribe. They therefore forcibly converted the Tutsi to Christianity; gave them positions of power in society and the labour force; gave them the power to inflict exploitative and punitive measures on the Hutu; and even made it so that education itself was only reserved for Tutsi children. All essentially leading to the poverty, famine, and oppression of the Hutu tribes. So now, by the time Rwanda regained its independence in 1962, the Hutu majority was thirsty for revenge, and so, in a burst of passion and destiny they burned down all Tutsi houses in numerous locations, sending some 300,000 of them into exile.

This was obviously only the beginning, however, as Keen further narrated quite expertly, "In 1994, militiamen from Rwanda's Hutu ethnic group had taken part in the murder of some 800,000 Rwandan citizens … When Tutsi rebels seized power in Rwanda and put a stop to the 1994 genocide, Hutu militias (ably assisted by France) took refuge in eastern DRC [Democratic Republic of Congo], where they were planning to resume their murderous campaign inside Rwanda." In like manner, there is an overlooked relation between these Rwandan/Congolese genocides and the current Israeli genocide of the Palestinians – if not, then at least their forcing them into the most desperate of apartheid-like conditions. On top of this, them behaving surprised, even shocked and victimised, when they responded to this mistreatment with violence. In all, these events further demonstrate how Death and Hades are being very well present, using both soft power and hard power to accomplish their genocidal ends.

Moreover, to further explain the horrific conditions the Palestinians have been living through in the OPT (Occupied Palestinian Territory), Imseis spoke of the "massive influx of Israeli settlers into the OPT, causing their numbers to more than double, from some 200,000 to well over 400,000; the rapid construction of hundreds of kilometers of additional *settler-only* bypass roads connecting the settlements with Israel; the presence of some 200 Israeli *military bases/posts* throughout the OPT; the erection of the wall; the destruction of the Palestinian village-road network; and the imposition of a complex regime of closures, curfews, and a South-Africa style 'permit system' that severely limited Palestinian freedom of movement. As a result, the Palestinian inhabitants of the West Bank were confined in '227 non-contiguous islands,' and the Palestinians of the Gaza Strip were left to fester in one of the most densely populated and impoverished places on earth. According to the U.N. special rapporteur on human rights in the OPT, John Dugard, this situation led to the development of 'an apartheid regime worse than the one that existed in South Africa'" (Imseis 2010: 271; emphasis mine).

All this, to me, looks eerily close to the systematic erasure and removal of a people from their own land (or perhaps from the face of the earth), while claiming just and noble reasons for such a desire. The truth is, it is impossible to truly understand a people, a movement, or an insurgency until you consider its context. What most people have done, and in the case of Rwanda did, was throw these things off to ethnic squabblings. Indeed, to add a further justification the Israelis used the hugely emotive and demonising spectre of "Terrorist" to thereby cement what support they could gather from any potential stragglers. Hereby, to give a more comprehensive understanding to you, and to show the absolute bankruptcy of such a loaded and overused term, I will first detach it from its current relation and identification with Islam and Islamism; then I will hopefully be able to demystify its usage.

First, in order to detach the word "terrorist" from the word Islamist, or even fundamentalist, we must start by removing the blatant lie that Islamism is a late modern form of fascism. The following spectrum presented here is a non-biased and non-prejudiced spectrum of the various big ideological movements of the last three centuries. From left to right they are: anarchism (the furthest left), then ecologism (or the green movement), then communism, then socialism, then queerism, then feminism, then liberalism. These are the main left-wing movements. Moving on, again, from left to right: conservatism, *then fundamentalism*, then nationalism, then imperialism, then fascism, then Nazism. It is the most irresponsible of narrations and storytellings to equate and associate Islamism (a form of fundamentalism) with fascism (an oppressive, elitist, corporatist, brutalist, and imperialist form of police-statism), but that is what is currently done in many Western media, especially in the US.

To give further reference, virtually every one of those ideologies have, at some point in their history, a time when they themselves used or resorted to terrorism or to terroristic tactics in order to achieve their ideological vision. The anarchists post-Bakunin were known for using terrorist tactics to destabilise governments. The green movement has had a history of eco-terrorists and "green warriors" who have practiced what could be called "terrorism lite" as their attacks damaged property or freed wildlife but rarely killed anybody.

Communism's early history was one of terror, prior to Marx it was conspiratorial terrorism, attacking the governments of France and other Europeans locations, post-Marx communism was more about large masses led by Marxist or vanguard leaders. The early socialists could also be said to have used "terrorism lite" in that they bombed or disrupted factories, buildings, offices, derailed train tracks, and otherwise obstructed production, but very few people got hurt. And as I am not excessively familiar with all the ins-and-outs of either the queer or the feminist movements I will have to say that perhaps neither of them, of all these ideologies, ever engaged in any terrorist atrocities to get their message across, but I am fine with being proved wrong about that. As for the liberals, they have one of the most notorious histories of all with regard to terrorism, the Jacobin Great Terror, in which anyone showing any sign of monarchical attachment could literally get their head chopped off.

For the record, however, none of this means the Right has been excessively innocent in all this either. The history of conservative terrorism is a lot more nuanced. In English history the terrorism of Henry VIII against the Catholics and of Mary Tudor in response are legend. Then there was the further terrorism of King James I against the non-conformists (ultimately leading many of them to immigrate to Holland, and then from Holland to the New World). As to American conservative terrorists, I hopefully have no need to remind White America of the Salem Witch Trials, the existence of the Klan, and various other White supremacist groups, or of the terror inflicted by McVeigh and his like.

With regard to fundamentalist terror it is already well known from the side of the Islamist, however, what a lot of people in our time somehow fail to appreciate is that Zionism is also just as much a fundamentalist movement (cloaked and protected by European and American interests) as Islamism, mercilessly getting away with their numerous terrorist atrocities against the Palestinian people. Indeed, if we were now to consider "the question of Israel: how it was able to displace and obliterate the Palestinian presence and the fact that the Palestinians never stopped resisting their imposed fate or devising counter-strategies, of which the one-state solution was the one ... most strongly advocated ... Of course, [this] simple, largely agricultural people with poor education and modest political aspiration had been forced into close proximity with a formidable foe: European Jews allied to European imperialism, who were imbued with a 'yearning for Jewish political and religious self-determination ... to be exercised on the promised land." This has effectively all been accomplished through Israel's use and exploitation of both hard and soft power.

With regard to nationalism, we could, with no ill or undue malice intended, remember that many anti-colonial struggles used terrorism in the early parts of their liberation movements to fight against the settlers. Also, the IRA's (Irish Republican Army's) use of terrorist tactics to achieve their vision of a fully unified and independent Ireland is even to this day the stuff of legend. As to imperialism I hopefully will not need to remind you of the track record of imperialist violence and terror all over Africa, in India, and in Latin America. With regard to fascism there were, to my personal knowledge, only three solidly fascist states: Italy, Spain, and Japan. Of these, Italy used terror on the Ethiopians, Spain used terror on the anarchists, and Japan intended to inflict a level of terror, or at least mass violence, on China and America. Indeed, the Kamikaze fighters no doubt used a form of terrorism against the US.

Finally, Nazi terrorism should not need to be excessively dwelt upon, but we should remember that the deaths that occurred during World War II reached as high as 85 million overall of those who died, directly or indirectly, as a result of Nazism; 50 million civilian deaths; 25 million military deaths; 5 million prisoner of war (POW) deaths; 11 million Soviet civilian deaths; 10 million Soviet concentration camp deaths (i.e. Holocaust deaths); and 6 million World War II related Soviet deaths in the postwar period. Not to mention 3 million Chinese military deaths; 8 million Chinese civilian deaths; and 5-10 million World War II related Chinese deaths in the postwar period.

All this, in total, puts the Soviet and Chinese deaths caused by Nazism to be 27-28 million among the Soviets and 16-21 million among the Chinese. All to go with the estimated 6-7 million Ashkenazi Jews, 250 thousand disabled people, 100-200 thousand Freemasons, and 10 thousand homosexuals that died during the Holocaust. To be clear, the Ashkenazim were not the only victims of the Holocaust, they were not even the largest number of those brutally murdered during the Holocaust (that title goes to the Soviets at an estimated 10 million), nor the first to be placed into concentration camps (another title going to the communists, this time predominantly German). In sum, World War II was a global war with global proportions. Thus, no one community has the right to claim they suffered more or worse from Nazi terrorism than any others. The world suffered from Nazi terrorism.

What I hope I have hereby achieved is the successful detachment of terrorism from its current connection to fundamentalism and Islamism. Also to have at least slightly contributed to the weakening or lessening of its use to justify all manner of atrocious acts against Muslim nations, each fighting against what they believe to be – not necessarily American decadence, as is so often believed by most Western narrators – American imperialism, European orientalism, and Zionist annexationism. One of the major problems with creating simplistic, threatening, and villainous daemons like the "terrorist" has perhaps been expressed best by the words of Keen: "an overt and publicly expressed intention to defeat [any] demon enemy – whether RUF rebels in Sierra Leone or the Viet Cong in Vietnam or the Taliban in Afghanistan – has repeatedly created huge opportunities for diverse actors within the counterinsurgency to engage in politically and economically advantageous abuse with minimal international criticism."

Again, it could be said that Death uses national soft power to blind the international community to the truths of what is really going on in the world. All thus bringing us back again to Rwanda, "The Rwandan regime had considerable international sympathy that had been encouraged by collective guilt over the international community's non-response to the 1994 genocide. But this guilt was now feeding renewed suffering – and some began to talk of new genocides *within the DRC*, including mass mortality among the Hutu refugee population. Hundreds of thousands were deprived of humanitarian relief, and in 1996-97 an estimated 232,000 Hutu refugees were killed in the DRC, primarily at the hands of the Rwandan army and its Congolese rebel ally, the Alliance of Democratic Forces for the Liberation of Congo (ADFL)." Moreover, the Hutu/Tutsi genocide continues on, even to this day, in the DRC, and shows little sign of abating. Soft power thus has the ability to vocalise certain voices while muting and silencing others. This is what ultimately makes it so useful to conceptual entities like Death and Hades.

All that being said, there is still an argument to be made, which the prophet Ezekiel would delineate prophetically in one of his earlier scrolls, that Death was in fact, and has been this whole time, a being both subservient to, and in the service of, Allah himself for the purpose of removing systems that he was ready to judge: "Though Noah, Daniel, and Job, were in [a land], as I live, saith the Lord God, they shall deliver their own souls by their righteousness. For thus saith the Lord God; How much more when I send my four sore judgments upon Jerusalem, the sword, and the famine, and the noisome beast, and the pestilence, to cut off from it man and beast?"

Effectively, we can find here the ways of Allah, that he sometimes uses Death and Hades to bring an entity to its ultimate manifestation. True indeed, each of these last four horsemen: War, Famine, Death, and Hades could even turn out to be the mysterious four angels "bound in the great river Euphrates" (9: 14) that had been prepared for that very hour, and day, and month, and year. Therefore, while I personally theorise that the first horseman is most likely the Great Witness from al-Khidr, destined to bring plague and pestilence upon the earth; the four horsemen that follow him or her are far more likely to symbolise the four sore judgments Allah intends to inflict upon the earth nearing the end of his or her testimony.

Herein we can also appreciate how difficulties like death exist in virtually every entity imaginable, to carry them through into their next manifestation. The death of an entity is thereby its transitioning from one state to another in manifestation. Non-existence in itself is actually an absurdity. All things have life as all things have energy. Energy, that is, interactive desire and motion, exists everywhere and in all things, and it can never die. All it does is merely change from one state to another. The same is also true of the human soul. It does not actually die, in the sense of ceasing to be, it merely transitions from one form of existence to another. In this, we understand the Day of the Lord to actually be a time of severe change, when the world shall meet Allah face to face, and shall therefore be changed. Even the apostle Paul said of it "the dead shall be raised incorruptible, and we shall be changed."

But the changing of the world has occurred many times historically: the latest being the rise of modernity. Yet modernism will also have to stand face to face with Death, being, in actuality, nothing more than a European version of Americanism. American neo-colonialism has thus been backed and supported by European idealists who understand that the system itself currently stands by the power and dominance of American imperialism. All nations that are subject to the White House, IMF, World Bank, US Treasury, and USAID (which all make up the current Washington consensus) are all subjects to the GUSE (Great United States Empire) and to US neo-colonialism. By transcending modernism, one effectively transcends the imperial seat of the US and may even rouse their displeasure. True indeed, Europe is not officially subjected to the US as such, but they have still surrendered their power to its empire, as they too follow the modernist agenda.

The intellectual fight back of the twentieth century led up to postmodernism; but modernism was only really triumphed here. Nonetheless modernity reaches its full demise only when a new system, like thearchism, has become the new establishment, leaving liberalism behind to the darkness. This kind of revolution will set off a true postmodernism. It will also put in place a new standard for living and perceiving. When philosophical movements have reached their height then comes a tipping point at which time anything can set off revolution. The main motivating force behind modernism was humanism. We need a new motivating system in place of humanism's failed mission to improve our lot. While, true indeed, Existentialism seems to be the motivating force behind the current school of post-modernism, it cannot account for the pneumatological realities that exist within the universe. Herein is where the movement of thearchism becomes seriously interesting.

If we consider one of modernism's greatest strengths it would be its monopoly on intellectual/scientific representation. It seems all intellectual and scientific achievement flows directly from modernists and modernisers. The inferiorising of ancient customs and traditions, the rejecting and neglecting of what is essentially real and true subjectively to other races and people, has brought about the humiliation of tribal knowledge, secrets, and remedies and the glorification of all Western sciences. As concepts like race begin to get triumphed by ethnicity so the concept of modernity is slowly getting triumphed by an anti-modern movement. But anti-modernism should not be a shift back to a past nirvana, it should be a shift into a bright interdependent future. It should recall nature in that all natural beings know their place in nature and operate within that sphere. This more naturalistic future is based on demodernisation into something less intellectually based.

But as any true postmodernism brings on the death pangs of modernism — a system centred on liberalism — such an actuality may seem contemptuous, even blasphemous, to most modern minds. The movement from the rule of law to the rule of Allah means a transition from liberalism to thearchism must occur. True indeed, far from creating a world of freedom, liberalism has only produced an oppression to surveillance, all in the name of security. Not giving people the freedom to rule themselves is the only way that liberalism can actually ensure that it does not collapse into the pernicious malaise of chaos. This is the psychologic of self-disclosed humanity: not the freedom of humanism but the oppression of dehumanisation. Here liberalism is not the aspiration of subjected humanity but the imposition of modernist effectuation.

Ultimately, what we can conclude here is that Death, having been sent out also to conquer, was not meant to be taken literally, in the physical sense of the idea, but was considered an individual experience we all receive when we come to understand death as an inevitability, a prelude to elevation we all must go through. Here, Death, though preparing for the great battle of the Day of Allah, is also the very messenger of Allah sent to bring humanity to the point of reaching divinity. Thereby, the warfare between Death and Allah, is really just a ruse for the true warfare between the nations and Allah. If there was no fight before, there is definitely about to be one now.

"Fear Not They Which Can Destroy the Body"

At the point when the Lamb opened the fifth seal (6: 9-11) the souls (*psychikos*) of those who were unjustly murdered for the sake of Allah and for their testimony cried out to Allah for justice, for vengeance, and for revenge. It is here that Death and Hades, having already prepared for warfare, and having gathered and assembled their various armies and their captives, appear to have been challenging the very sovereignty of the Messiah. Basically, having already conquered and overcome every principality and power of the astral plane, the Messiah was clearly now preparing to conquer and overcome every government and territory of the physical plane – the last perhaps being that of Death himself. It could be, or at least was very likely hoped to have been, that by his conquering of Death the Messiah would thereby have crystallised all his victories; lest having overcome in both the astral and the physical he end up surrendering them all to Death.

Therefore the stage was now fully set for the great battle of Death and Hades; even as the prophet Isaiah exclaimed in his own scroll of apocalypses: "And in this mountain shall the Lord of hosts make unto all people a feast of fat things, a feast of wines well refined. And he will destroy in this mountain the face of the covering cast over all people, and the veil that is spread over all nations. He will swallow up death in victory; and the Lord God will wipe away tears from all faces; and the rebuke of his people shall he take away from off all the earth: for the Lord hath spoken it."

The Messiah's final victory over Death would thereby allow for the freeing of the captives belonging to both Death and Hades, and the clothing of them with the clothing of Allah's people. The white robes given to them were to symbolise a sealing of righteousness and give them a place among those who would come later, at the opening of the sixth seal. These suffering and executed martyrs were here clothed in what were essentially white *djellabas* and white abayas, each of them washed in the bleach of the blood of the Lamb. There was believed in this gesture to have been found enough satisfaction to help them overcome the adversity and captivity they were then suffering. These symbols would have all been seen as images of hope to the messianic communities that were enduring persecution from the then Imperial State.

But persecution from imperial powers is nothing new, the scrolls of Daniel and the scrolls of Maccabeus are filled with them. Yet our hope takes on new bounds when we return again to the prophet Ezekiel's astral drama, "Thou shalt fall upon the mountains of Israel, thou, and all thy bands, and the people that is with thee: I will give thee unto the ravenous birds of every sort, and to the beasts of the field to be devoured. Thou shalt fall upon the open field: for I have spoken it, saith the Lord God. And I will send a fire on Magog, and among them that dwell carelessly in the isles: and they shall know that I am the Lord." However, within our modern situation a new level of persecution and torture through psychological methodologies, deserves some significant recognition. The growing reality within colonial systems, and within the current neo-colonial manifestation of the GUSE, is that torture is inescapable so as to maintain political hegemony. But whereas in ancient times they tortured the body and put the body through the extremities of physiological pain, now they torture the mind and create ever newer means of psychological pain.

The political and, indeed, philosophical dimensions of modern torture reveal that the problem is deeper than the use of implements to cause pain; it is found in the ruling ideas of the imperial state. Acculturation methods, with the ruse of integration hopes, are applied to foreign countries with the distinct expectation of isolating and removing any form of political challenge to the imperialist agenda. Disciplining of any defiance to the imperial doctrine is, of course, the essential aim of the neo-colonial state. However, the use of torture under the pretext of what Lou Turner called "enhanced interrogation techniques" for the purpose of coercing compliant behaviour, calls the ethical superiority of the entire imperial edifice into question.

To further explain the realities of the tortured Turner spoke of how, "To break down his resistance, police or military personnel arbitrarily round up ten to a dozen local residents and torture five or six of them to death while the suspected insurgent observes. After several homicidal tortures, the real interrogation begins. According to this method, torture, indeed murder, is used as an agent to condition the response of a detainee and also as a ruse for the dual concealment of the official nonknowing of intelligence and the possible knowing of official nonknowing by insurgents." These extremes to which the state is willing to go to maintain its form of hegemony are problematic as they do more to radicalise individuals than police them. At the same time, torture is a standard procedure within the context of any warfare. Thereby, with this legitimation tactic the use of such enhanced interrogation methods to break *suspected* resistance in fighting their Wars on Terror, Wars on Drugs, Wars on Crime, and various other nondescript wars becomes de-problematised.

Fanon took the argument even further by breaking down the forms of torture used by the imperial power during liberation struggles such as what occurred in Algeria. The first category of torture he spoke of was, what he called "preventive tortures." "We here refer to brutal methods which are directed towards getting prisoners to speak rather than to actual torture. The principle that over and above a certain threshold pain becomes intolerable takes on here singular importance. The aim is to arrive as quickly as possible at that threshold." In these cases, Fanon explained, the interrogator would use methods such as, "Injection of water by the mouth accompanied by an enema of soapy water given at high pressure"; "Introduction of a bottle into the anus"; and "Two forms of torture called 'motionless torture' in which the interrogated are placed in incomprehensible positions requiring movement but should such movement occur they are instantly attacked."

Fanon further articulated how the repercussions of using such methods on some people, who, "Being tortured night and day for nothing seemed to have broken something in these men. One of these sufferers had a particularly painful experience. After some days of useless torturing, the police came to realize that they were dealing with a peaceable man who knew nothing whatever about anybody in an F.L.N. network. In spite of being convinced of this, a police inspector had said: 'Don't let him go like that. Give him a bit more, so that when he gets out he'll keep quiet.'" Clearly, the man was already broken and there was no need for any added humiliation, however, power rarely cares for the needs or pains of those it inflicts with suffering.

Fanon also spoke of a third form of torture, which came about through the imperialist collusion with the medical establishment, "When dealing with a patient who seems to suffer from an unconscious inner conflict which consultations do not manage to exteriorize, the doctor has recourse to chemical methods of exploration. Pentothal, given by intravenous injection, is the most common serum used to liberate the patient of a conflict which seems to be beyond his powers of adaptation." Yet, if with "neurosis pentothal sweeps away the barriers which bar the way to bringing to light an interior conflict, it ought equally in the case of Algerian patriots to serve to break down the political barrier and make confession easier for the prisoner without having recourse to electricity; [even as] medical tradition lays down that suffering should be avoided".

This technique was extremely deceptive, as, though it appeared to be saving the tortured from the physical threat of more severe forms of torture, such as electricity, it still produced psychological traumata within the minds of its victims. Fanon explained that what would happen as a result of using this typology of interrogation was that "the patient [would] not even know whether he has given any information away. [Thus, the] sense of culpability towards the cause he was fighting for and his brothers in arms whose names and addresses he may have given here weighs so heavily as to be dramatic. No assurance can bring peace to these broken consciences." Still, such extreme forms of modern interrogation do bear modest similarities to the forms of torturing used against the early messianic movement during the days of Roman imperialism. These tactics were all applied in the hopes of coercing from the disciple a renunciation of the Messiah and of the kingdom of God.

Then again, if we consider the more up-to-date Black American struggle of our own time: as a result of the hopes generated by the Civil Rights movement and the few wins that had transpired therefrom, many Black people believed that the hegemonic powers were finally starting to concede defeat. However, Huey Newton and the Black Panther Party of the 1960s-80s were not in the least deceived by White supremacy's weakened, yet completely unconquered, position. Singh exclaimed concerning their situation that "even as the legal edifice of segregation was being dismantled by government decree, a much more enduring structure of 'spatial apartheid' had been made visible by its inscription into the urban landscape. In this sense, the vision of the ghetto as an internal colony, or perhaps better, a neocolony, was not simply an analogy. As James Blaut argues, although ghettos clearly lack the ability to press for self-determination as 'politico-geographic units,' [they actually] define the relations of exploitation and oppression that govern relations with dominant power. These relations, moreover, are defined in rigid, socio-spatial terms, because ghettoized/colonized areas are excluded from sharing in social/global surpluses."

Nevertheless, ghetto culture as it stands today is no culture at all; it is in fact capitalism on a hyper and massive scale. Their clothes are more expensive and so are their cars; their jewellery is bigger and their home accessories are flashier. Pretty much everything they buy has to be great or hyped up. It is a hypercapitalism to the extreme. Therefore, for the sake of thearchy we of the godbody culture have for the most part come to see that ghetto capitalist culture is not representative of our reality or of our desire. Effectively, even as Black Panther leader Linda Harrison also said:

> "We have no culture but a culture born out of our resistance to oppression. 'No colonial system draws it justification from the fact that the territories [and people] it dominates are culturally nonexistent. You will never make colonialism blush for shame by spreading out little known cultural treasures under its eyes' (quoted from The Wretched of the Earth)."

So, our counter-culture as a godbody movement must, of necessity, be an anarcho-Islamism even as the current culture of the GUSE has decayed into a Christo-fascist culture. With the devolution of Charismatic Prosperity Theology into a Christo-fascist ideology the dangers ahead are that this Christo-fascism is not only manifesting among the American Republicans but even among the American Democrats. This danger, however, is not from the people as such, but from the leaders, who, for the most part, have adopted the Charismatic view that the inerrancy of the Bible means that only the prosperous are blessed of God, and that any disabled, sick, physically, mentally, or financially othered grouping or person is obviously cursed or abandoned by God. Moreover, with America being the wealthiest, strongest, most powerful nation in its own eyes, God is thereby obviously with them as a people and as a country.

But these Christo-fascist tendencies have existed in America for years. According to Hayes and Kiene, "In the late 1960s, the Black Panther Party gained national attention as an organization of defiant young Black men and women committed to resisting by any means necessary what Malcolm X had called America's White power structure [i.e. White fascist tendencies]. Emerging within the crucible of the Black power movement, these urban revolutionaries symbolized the rejection of Martin Luther King, Jr., and the civil rights establishment's sterile theorizing and ineffectual strategies of nonviolent civil disobedience in the Northern setting. Viewing urban Black communities as colonies occupied by a system of hostile White police, the Panthers fearlessly contested the power of the state to brutalize Black citizens." Indeed, Singh also contributed that, "In developing their [own] brand of 'third worldism,' the Panthers turned to what was by far their most important ideological resource, the writings of Frantz Fanon."

Herein, what we can understand is that Fanon was a major influence on the Panthers in their desire to resist American neo-colonialist annexation. Essentially, "Although he [did employ the] Marxian theory of revolutionary change, Fanon [still] pointed out that it had to be sufficiently refashioned to fit the colonial situation. He contended that anticolonial insurrection emerged in the countryside and filtered into the cities by means of the peasantry or the [underclass] who resided at the urban periphery" (Hayes & Kiene 2005: 160). This aspect of Panther theory, their alliance and siding with the underclass – their considering them to be the revolutionary section of society – was new and powerful. It instilled in the ghetto people a sense of destiny away from the streets. They could see that they were on a mission against a powerful and unbeatable behemoth, a Great United States Empire (GUSE) that cared nothing for them and took few prisoners.

Obviously, for those who have not read Fanon, he is not for the faint of heart. Indeed, like myself, he is and can be a very difficult read for many, particularly those from the hood (ghetto), who for the most part are, if not uneducated, usually undereducated. According, again, to Singh, "Fanon's relevance was by no means immediately evident to the Panthers themselves. David Hilliard, for example, candidly recalls the feelings of self-loathing and futility brought on by his many frustrating attempts to make sense of Fanon's complex prose. Yet Hilliard also tells of his perseverance and increasing excitement as he began to understand new concepts and ways of thinking about the Black experience in America in the discussions of Fanon's writings in the Party's political education classes." Again, through Fanon the Panthers were able to see the relevance of the frequent ghetto uprisings that were transpiring in those days as the spontaneous violence of the colonised fighting against their colonisation.

Moreover, Singh further continued, "The Black Panther Party, though it never developed a comprehensive urban theory or strategy … was nevertheless the product of [an] emergent understanding of the socio-spatial logic and politics of ghettoization. Once again seizing upon Fanon's work for appropriate concepts, the Panthers emphasized the colonizing, as opposed to the strictly national aspects of ghettoization, and identified Fanon's lumpen proletarian [underclass] as a ghetto archetype and the most 'spontaneously revolutionary' agent of the Black struggle in the overdeveloped world." It would be through this theoretical basis that the Panthers were able to find connections between the liberation struggles going on in Vietnam, Latin America, and parts of Africa, effectively, the colonised world or so-called Third World, and the liberation struggle going on in the urban streets of Oakland, Chicago, New York City, and Boston. Through neo-colonialism, what should have simply been urbanisation, became to Black America ghettoisation.

Based on this understanding and outlook the US police were not seen as protectors or keepers of the peace but as a colonialist troop sent to the ghettos of the GUSE to undermine any radical resistance. In effect, through their studying and understanding of Fanon, the Panthers could perceive the coming of "urban revolt [and so] embraced the Black ghetto as the basis of a renewed and very different kind of Black radical vision: the site of a radically dispersed Black nation and the model of the internal colonization of America's Black people. Reappropriating ghettoized spaces from the pathologizing discourse of social science, Black liberation politics instead figured the ghetto as a place of 'irredeemable *spatial* difference' within the nation-state, irrecuperable to unifying temporal narratives of national belonging and citizenship."

Based on this narrative of national citizenship police officers, as a manifestation of the national-state, currently claim their authority is due to their duty and obligation to protect all US communities, further claiming that they will only enter and patrol them in a respectful manner and for their own safety. But they prove they are not obliged to make any Black communities feel safer or they would stop arresting and murdering innocent Black lives for such simple things as playing with toys or sleeping in their beds. They are actually making only one group of people feel safer in this society, White people. But who are they saving White people from?

As any keen observer would be able to put together, the police are sent to our communities to protect White people from the frustration and disillusionment of the underclass. In order to reach the many with the order of the few, terror, intimidation, brutality, and murder are the tactics the police use and have been using. Who suffers? You and I suffer. To them we are the ones that may get out of line; we are the ones that may rage against our exploitation; we are the ones with a revolutionary tendency and nothing to lose by fighting them. In the long run, the police, as pawns in this modern bourgeois society will be the main force used to block any movement within our communities by arresting any members of our communities that show any signs of nonconformity.

Even so, within the current underclass has arisen the super-gangster movement. Having myself been a member of the movement's foundational gang, the Crips, I can say with all honesty, I loved being a Crip. It is for this reason that I believe, not only does Pantherism, but even super-gangsterism, has and have something incredible to offer to godbodyism. While, true indeed, the philosophy, ideology, and lessons of the godbody are without doubt unquestionable. At the same time, the super-gang culture and lifestyle is definitely worth emulating. Here I would like to encourage my godbody brothers and sisters to seek to form an alliance with the super-gangsters, thereby we can both learn from and move with each other as two powerful underclass movements.

True, we, the underclass, currently fill up the jails and prisons of America, whether by bad or good "citizens." Prison as a whole, however, is filled with three kinds of "criminals": those who are inherently incorrigible and anti-social, who commit crimes for nothing but the rush; those that Huey Newton called "illegitimate capitalists," who have conformed to the ideas and ideals of the system but see no legitimate means of survival within it but to break its laws; and finally, political prisoners, who have a major problem with the system and its ideals and take direct actions to change or challenge it, it is this action that landed them in prison.

Illegitimate capitalists and political prisoners can be either apologists or fanatics based on their state of mind. For example, a terrorist in prison may think what they have done was right, they are political prisoners, but their thinking is fanatical. However, there are terrorists that seek to explain their actions and justify them to those outside of their circle, these are apologists for themselves and others like them, either way a terrorist is a political prisoner, even though they should be punished for the evil of what they did.

Furthermore, on the subject of snitching, two very important points must be understood immediately: (i) Snitching only applies to those who use government power, force, and institutions to punish, persecute, or otherwise profit from someone belonging to one of those second two categories of "criminal" mentioned earlier. (ii) A woman using the same government power, force, or institutions against a rapist, paedophile, physical abuser, child abuser, or a man that literally shot her in a car, is hardly a snitch. She is a survivor. If we must employ terminologies like snitch and informer, which I believe we should, we must not dilute their meaning by using them against innocent women that survived traumatic horrors and experiences we could never possibly understand being perpetrated against them by those they trusted.

Effectively, prison is supposed to be for the anti-social, but anti-sociality can come in many forms. The most obvious is violating the law. Moreover, one who is anti-social and commits a crime in their anti-sociality does deserve to be punished for it, even though the penitentiary system can itself be a form of psychological torture in its own right. See, the modern state exists as the only body that holds a legitimate monopoly on violence; and the most prominent symbol of state violence, in our time, is the penitentiary system. Prior to the founding of the penitentiary in the 18th century the symbols of state violence were the whip and the chain.

Prisons, at that time, were merely holding facilities before trial; and punishments were usually state orchestrated corporal punishments such as beatings, amputations, mutilations, placement in the stocks, or being drawn. Having a monopoly on all legitimate violence meant, back then, that these acts of state-sponsored violence were public spectacles that would leave a flesh wound on the body, hence, the name corporal. However, around the 1750s many reformists believed that a more civilised form of punishment would be the carceral form, where people could be put in a quiet location to think about what they had done and the harm they had caused. This, it was believed, would lead to penitence and thereby reform the convicted into an upstanding citizen.

Since those days carceral punishment has become not only legitimised but normalised. Even to the point that society is unable and unwilling to think of non-carceral measures of dealing with deviance. The strongest case for carceral punishment comes from the carceral feminists who say that men who abuse or rape women must be locked away and kept from harming others in the future. This legitimation of carceral punishment fails to see passed the societal gendering of prisons as male or to appreciate the nightmare of female incarceration. True, there is a far greater quantity of males incarcerated. Still, those women that do get locked up face many problematic scenarios as a result of their sentencing.

Even before their sentencing women have to face the sexual abuse of the strip search, in which officers and nurses search every cavity of their bodies: vagina, anus, and mouth, with their fingers. Male officers have even been known to grope vaginas, chests, and buttocks in sexually suggestive ways while on duty; and these are regular occurrences for women in jails and prisons. On top of that, there are the numerous reports of sexual harassment and vaginal, anal, and oral rape from correction officers. More importantly, they are unable to escape from their abusers, being imprisoned by them. I can attest from my own experience on Rikers, correction officers were well known for taking advantage of inmates' vulnerable position to acquire sexual favours from them. This is due to public unawareness and officer vilification of the inmates, hypersexualising and fetishising them.

But we still have not addressed the fear of the carceral feminists. What do we do with all the rapists and paedophiles? This is a loaded question, but it is also a misconception of the situation. These labels used to dehumanise and demonise these people allow us to forget that everybody has a shadow side, and we are all capable of untold atrocities given the right circumstances. By demonising these people as inherently evil and not the victims of circumstances that occurred in their lives to corrupt them, we fail to notice or deal with what creates rapists and paedophiles. Herein, the problem is not the individual (as in them being inherent evil), the problem is in the current system of modernity.

The very popular copaganda circulating throughout society is that prisons are to protect "good people" from the "bad people," usually coded as Black people. This creates the idea that prison is only filled with those who deserve punishment. The police, therefore, like your typical Marvel superhero, save innocent people from these "evil villain" ghetto people. This black and white way of thinking couples the idea of the Black criminal with that of the supervillain and not with that of the misled or misguided human being, capable just as much of good as they have been of negativity. Thereby it also justifies the state's and the law enforcer class' monopoly on violence as ordinary people are potentially too evil to be allowed to use violence at their own discretion.

In all, to envision a world without state-sponsored violence we must first envision a world without the traumatising and distorting realities of carceral punishment. To do this we must now understand, with Angela Davis, that prisons will not be replaced by one all-encompassing solution but with several interconnected solutions. These solutions are: (i) decriminalising all currently illegal drugs and substances. To go with this the allowing of all users that wish to quit easy access to the best programmes and counselling, including Narcotics Anonymous, with which to do so. The example here would be American prohibition. By legalising all forms of alcohol, they put an end to those lucrative criminal enterprises and the mob violence they entailed.

(ii) Decriminalising all forms of consensual sexual performances, including: all forms of public nudity, all forms of consensual sexual public performances, and all forms of consensual sexual media performances. If a woman or a man chooses to provide any form of sexual favours with their own body as a compensation for a given product or service, such is their prerogative. Along with this, teaching, training, and guidance on sexual preferences, performances, and potentials should be provided to all young people as they mature, as well as guidance in sexual safety and contraceptives for all precoital, coital, and postcoital experiences. Finally, the institutions of marriage and divorce should also be abolished in the process, thereby allowing for new forms of relational and intimate interaction to be developed. All this will go a long way in eliminating the need or desire to rape or molest anybody.

(iii) Organising and establishing meeting grounds that are based on livelihood or employment within all neighbourhoods, workplaces, and universities to create social accountability, and to determine service capability. All this will go a long way in eliminating the need or desire to resort to deviant behaviours. (iv) Abolishing all forms of monetary compensation and monetary valuing. Compensation should thereby be through products and services, but the system itself should determine actual compensation through form of employment. All this will go a long way in eliminating the need or desire to steal anything. (v) Establishing a fighting ring as the new form of punitive justice, the rules of which can be decided by the community.

Now, the question: what about rapists and murderers seems somewhat moot. With the abolition of money and decriminalisation of all drugs there will be no reason to kill anybody. Also, with the decriminalisation of all forms of consensual sexual performative there will be no need to rape or molest anybody. With no monetary means of valuing products and persons no individual or group will feel their work is of higher or lower value than others. With punitive justice turned to a more humane form of corporal punishment than tortures, whippings, amputations, and mutilations the psychological trauma of internment and the hyperincarceration complex of the United States can be abolished. Again, prison and state abolition in our time is as unimaginable as slave trade and slave labour abolition were in their time, but it can definitely happen if we are willing to fight for it.

Furthermore, if we consider now the words of Abron, she perceived concerning the formative days of the Black Panther movement, "The 1966 version of the BPP ten-point Party platform included two demands concerning the United States criminal justice system. Point 8 demanded, 'We want freedom for all Black men held in federal, state, county, and city prisons and jails.' In a similar vein, Point 9 demanded, 'We want all black people when brought to trial to be tried in court by a jury of their peer group or people from their black communities, as defined by the Constitution of the United States.' In the early days of the organization, the Party informed community residents of their constitutional rights." These sorts of Panther initiatives allowed the Panthers to gain massive credibility in the Black communities of America, especially considering that the American government has always harassed and criminalised Black bodies.

Nevertheless, there is still in our time the hope for a new form of social organisation coming about in the global South. Especially in Africa, where modernist dreams have only become the disillusioned nightmare of repressed activism. US neo-colonialism and the American Christo-fascist order have set the pace for the agenda of Black people, whether in the continent or the diaspora. According to Nye, "More than four centuries ago, Niccolo Machiavelli advised princes in Italy that it was more important to be feared than to be loved. But in today's world, it is best to be both. Winning hearts and minds has always been important, but it is even more so in a global information age." Effectively, it is not enough to have military might and weaponry, not enough to have superior financial and technological capacities, not enough to have strategic and tactical advantage, if you are perceived to be unjust or oppressive you will still be hated, period.

To explicate this situation Nye provided the perfect evidential arguments, noting, "For example, in terms of resources the United States was far more powerful than Vietnam, yet we lost the Vietnam War. And America was the world's only superpower in 2001, but we failed to prevent September 11." It is for this cause that he also stated, "The United States may [currently] be more powerful than any other polity since the Roman Empire, but like Rome, America is neither invincible nor invulnerable. Rome did not succumb to the rise of another empire, but to the onslaught of waves of barbarians. Modern high-tech [Islamists] are the new barbarians." What he was saying was that it is important for America to read the signs, the writing on the wall. True, America has historically had numerous preachers, satirists, academics, activists, and politicians predicting their downfall. Maybe they really thought the end was near, maybe they just wanted to advise or humble America. Either way, America's true fall, if it is to ever have one, will be due to its lack of tact and subtlety in appreciating global perceptions of it.

The powerful American behemoth, oddly enough, in many cases, finds itself in conflict with much weaker, and much less technologically or strategically advanced peoples. Like the barbarians in the times of Rome, they seem embarrassingly outmatched and outgunned, yet in a lot of cases (shockingly, more than the American public are aware of) America loses either a decisive victory or an instrumental ally. But, how could any plucky, yet ambitious, country rival the Goliath that is America, especially on the military stage? Here, perhaps, the problem is in the question. Many of America's greatest defeats occur, not because they or their allies lose on the military stage, but because America is not perceived to be a noble player fighting for noble reasons on the global stage.

America is unfortunately perceived to be, as stated in the original question, a Goliath. It is an effectively overpowered monster in the eyes of most people, therefore worthy of getting its head chopped off. Again, the perception of America, to the outside world, is based largely on how America perceives itself, but is subverted in all the areas where it would want the opposite. It is this subversion that distorts most people's views of America's intentions in many ways. What do I mean? Since the 1950s, America has been becoming a global force and participating in the global conversation. Moreover, they have also sought, sometimes covertly, sometimes overtly through force of arms, to overthrow any government that refuses to submit to them. They have also forced any government that *is* willing to submit to do so either monetarily or contractually. To the American people and their government these may all seem to reinforce their idea of "American exceptionalism," but outside of

America they are seen as demonstrations of political bullying, deceptive bribery, self-interested greed, media manipulation, and the spreading of immoral consumerism.

This image is more outside of Western spaces than within them. The problem in these situations is not that the ideal of America is not loved: an ideal represented in things like sports; Hollywood; hip hop, and most Black music genres; Amazon and most other online companies; social media and digital media; Smartphones and smart technology; AI and ML; and the various American counter-cultures. This America really resonates with most people all over the world. But juxtapose that with the American government, then it all goes pear-shaped. Many non-Americans would literally rather die than allow the American State to get even a foothold in their country, regardless of the political and economic benefits that could be gained.

From this premise we can see why most non-Americans currently believe that all the martyrs and saints that they see and know are suffering – or may have even lost their own lives, fighting to overthrow this system (that is itself understood by them to be a neo-colonialist monolith) – will one day bring about the eventual *eschaton* of this very system. Many of those victims of the current American Christo-fascist order, are, and have usually been, Islamic in orientation; some of them are *even today* still suffering in torture facilities as a result of the former War on Islam. We must therefore come to understand that our victory in dismantling the various structures of modernity comes about, firstly, through intellectual debate. As all new systems start off in the philosophical realm and then organise into movements so as to bring about social change; even so our own theoretical system of mental and bodily decolonisation will have to continue as such until the time of thearchic activism, when warfare, both intellectual and possibly martial, will be unleashed.

Even so, there is, or at least once was, a tradition within the godbody movement that spoke of a legal and martial harassment that was to come later upon the Black community, and particularly upon the godbody communities. It was believed that this event would be instigated by the United States government eventually leading on to our internment, isolation, torture, and even attempted genocide. Well, such an event may be transpiring before our very eyes right now with the current persecution of Muslims throughout the United States. Yet even despite this tradition we in the godbody presently lack any formal or universally recognised doctrine of death; let alone an understanding of it or of its intricacies.

Not that this book intends to explain or unravel any of its mysteries. Nonetheless, as a contribution, or at least a beginning, so as to lead the way towards the future development of a much more comprehensive adaptation, this book suggests that we borrow and reimagine from the super-gang culture our own, "Divine Army Chant:"

> *"If I should die, feel no shame; my soul will enter,*
> *the astral plane.*
> *So put the peace sign, across my chest;*
> *and tell the parliament, I did my best."*

While this may be a rather simple, and even simplistic, chant, originally created by the Crips due to the ever present reality of death among those in the gang life; it still contains a lot more subtlety than we or they have ever appreciated. Therefore, at least as a beginning to a much more comprehensive and satisfying understanding on our part: of death, life, and the afterlife, it is here being suggested that we adopt this ritual to be expressed at the close of all our ciphers and parliaments. This should also hopefully prepare us for the development of an authentically godbody funerary interpretation, as a God or Goddess enters the astral plane to dwell among the ancestors as themselves now becoming one of the ancestors (regardless of the age when they pass).

The Prophet of Islam shared a similar eschatological vision with his own people. Here, the word we call tribulation in the English language is called *Fitnah* in the Arabic, and it is believed in Islam that there will be six *fitnahs*. The Prophet said, "Enumerate six signs which will occur in close proximity to the Hour – 1) my death; 2) the conquering of Constantinople; 3) death that will take you like the barber of sheep (takes hair from them); 4) an abundant flow of wealth until a man receives 100 dinar yet still remains dissatisfied; 5) a trial that will not leave a single house from the Arabs except that it enters it; 6) then there will be a truce between you and the children of the yellow ones." Each of these signs of the Hour could be called a *fitnah*. Moreover, they, to a degree, also coincide with the various signs of the times in early messianic beliefs.

Yet the Prophet also said, "Between the creation of Adam and the arrival of the Hour, there is no *Fitnah* greater than the Dajjaal." Again, as we stated earlier, the *Dajjal* is the Islamic Anti-Christ, so it was believed in Islam that the *Dajjal* would rise from among the "yellow ones" (symbolic in those days for the Caucasians) and make war with the Muslims. It was further believed that during this warfare he would come to sign a truce with them but would break it halfway in and go right back to war. All this would thus inspire the Messiah (*al-Masih*) to return and defeat the *Dajjal*, basically killing him and all the armies of those willing to go to war for him. What we see therefore is that Islam understood that the Messiah would return, and that there would be a Divine Parousia, but only after the Great Tribulation (or *Fitnah al-Akbar*).

Still, anyone who takes a stand against the iniquities and inequities of the modern system will always find themselves called into question or persecuted as a criminal or extremist for their troubles. This will invoke arrest, torture, or even murder at the hands of a state machine that is said to serve the people. Again, this state machine, being based on a two-party, bureaucratically run, demagogically mandated, chaotically reinforced mechanism; is able to repress and transgress in the name of freedom. Freedom, thus, has become a watered-down excuse and cover for persecution of dissension. Any opinion that runs counter to the hegemony of the GUSE and its modernist agenda is callously targeted for exclusion and tribulation. We know this for sure: US neo-colonialism, in its current form as globalisation, is everywhere prevalent. The GUSE has military bases in virtually every country on the planet. One thing is for certain, imperialism is very much so still alive in our world today.

The Voice that Shakes the Earth

Following the opening of the sixth seal (6: 12-7:17) great and wondrous cataclysms occurred both in the earth and in the heavens. All that could be shaken was shaken, that which was called "the wrath of the Lamb" was unleashed, and all people were held to account for the various sins they had perpetrated. The entirety is reminiscent of where it was written in the epistle to the Hebrews, "See that ye refuse not him that speaketh: for if they escaped not who refused him that spake on earth, much more shall not we escape, if we turn away from him that speaketh from heaven: Whose voice then shook the earth: but now he hath promised, saying, Yet once more I shake not the earth only, but also heaven" (Hebrews 12: 25, 26). It is herein that the great Day of Vengeance prayed for by the martyrs of Allah is finally revealed, and the Lamb will get his revenge for all the blood that had been spilt by the ungodly against his people.

It is also here that the astral vision foreseen by the prophet Ezekiel finally comes to its desperate conclusion: "And, thou son of man, thus saith the Lord God; Speak unto every feathered fowl, and to every beast of the field, Assemble yourselves, and come; gather yourselves on every side to my sacrifice for you, even a great sacrifice upon the mountains of Israel, that ye may eat flesh, and drink blood. Ye shall eat the flesh of the mighty, and drink the blood of the princes of the earth, of rams, of lambs, and of goats, of bullocks, all of them fatlings of Bashan." "And it shall come to pass in that day, that I will give unto Gog a place there of graves in Israel, the valley of the passengers on the east of the sea: and it shall stop the noses of the passengers: and there shall they bury Gog and all his multitude: and they shall call it The valley of Hamon-gog."

For even though these Scriptures ultimately confirmed the following word spoken beforehand by the prophet Zephaniah, "Hold thy peace at the presence of the Lord God: for the day of the Lord is at hand: for the Lord hath prepared a sacrifice, he hath bid his guests. And it shall come to pass in the day of the Lord's sacrifice, that I will punish the princes, and the king's children, and all such as are clothed with strange apparel" (Zephaniah 1: 7, 8); the people of the early messianic movement would most likely have interpreted all this to be both an exaggerated and a distorted representation of the Armageddon War. (For the Armageddon War was believed by many to be a coming struggle in which the Thearchists – which in our time would be referring to the Islamists – went into battle with what, at that time, was presumed to be the Hellenists (that is, the Greeks); but as we can see was really supposed to be the empire of Gog, the last imperial power, representing the Hellenic empire).

So again, who is the real Gog and where is the real Magog? To answer these questions, we must consider again the imperial power in the world today, the power most likely to be a hindrance to the coming of Allah and of his thearchy. As for the man Gog himself, he will actually be the person that drives the world forces into battle with the bringers of the thearchy. The astral and physical warfare that occurs as a result will therefore be eschatological, even to the point that the dead will not be given a proper funeral but will be left out in the streets for the animals and birds to devour. The early messianic movement experienced this kind of Crusade against them, perpetrated by

Nero Caesar when he began his imperial witch hunt of the early messianic communities.

The knowledge of governmental persecution was, again, very apparent to first century messianism, which faced death for their confession of devotion to messianic authority. In those days, the messianic movement was itself condemned as what we would call in our day a terrorist movement. The godbody movement of today has a similar restriction, we therefore will very likely face a similar attack from media onslaught to what they faced. Here tragedies like war, famine, death, and the spectre of Hades (hell), will all represent plagues sent by Allah to judge the world, and particularly the GUSE, for their persecution of us godbodies, particularly those of us that are Muslim. But before Allah can pass his final judgment on the world, he will first send out an astral being, with "the seal of the living God," for the purpose of sealing those he has preserved for glory.

The prophet Ezekiel gave an even clearer picture as to what effectively qualifies someone for such an honour, but this time in a completely different astral vision from the first, stating:

"He cried also in mine ears with a loud voice, saying, Cause them that have charge over the city to draw near, even every man with his destroying weapon in his hand. And, behold, six men came from the way of the higher gate, which lieth toward the north, and every man a slaughter weapon in his hand: and one man among them was clothed with linen, with a writer's inkhorn by his side: and they went in, and stood beside the brazen altar. And the glory of the God of Israel was gone up from the cherub, whereupon he was, to the threshold of the house. And he called to the man clothed with linen, which had the writer's inkhorn by his side; And the Lord said unto him, Go through the midst of the city, through the midst of Jerusalem, and set a mark upon the foreheads of the men that sigh and that cry for all the abominations that be done in the midst thereof. And to the others he said in mine

hearing, Go ye after him through the city, and smite: let not your eye spare, neither have ye pity: slay utterly old and young, both maids, and little children, and women: but come not near any man upon whom is the mark; and begin at my sanctuary" (Ezekiel 9: 1-6).

Obviously, there are many who will disdain this type of language and instantly think, "How do we know the mark on those who mourned and cried for Jerusalem is not, in fact, the mark of the Beast?" For anyone with this sort of question I have given it a greater treatment in chapter 15. For now, however, know that the language is of very little significance. The mark on those who wept and mourned in Jerusalem is not likely to be the mark of the Beast as Allah does not tend to condemn those that are suffering. In fact, the Messiah said that such were blessed, saying, "Blessed are they that mourn: for they shall be comforted" (Matthew 5: 4). Hereby, the mark spoken of here, in the context of the prophet Ezekiel's vision, is in fact very likely to be the seal of the living God, in the context of the apostle John's vision.

This seal was to be a sign and proof of affiliation to the people of Allah, given to those who, like those that mourned at the abominations of Jerusalem, look at the world today and hunger and thirst for a day when it will actually be righteous. Essentially, the seal of Allah was understood to be more than merely an awkward mysticism or some backward traditionalism, but a transcending of both mysticism and traditionalism. Indeed, the stuff that dreams are made of. For even as Queen Makeda of Sheba said in Solomon's Song of Songs, "Set me as a seal upon thine heart, as a seal upon thine arm: for love is strong as death; jealousy is cruel as the grave: the coals thereof are coals of fire, which hath a most vehement flame" (Song of Solomon 8: 6). Yet the Hebrew word used here for love was the word *ahab*, which, though, true indeed, can be defined as love, is not so much the love a person has for their friend or sibling, nor even the love a soldier has for their people. *Ahab* mainly, though not exclusively, denoted love in the libidinal sense, as in romantic love.

On the other hand, the Hebrew word used here for jealousy was the word *qinah*, a word that actually comes from the root word *qana*, and means zeal or passion, not jealousy in the sense of wanting what someone else has, or bitterness over a lover's so-called betrayal. It only got mistranslated as jealousy due to a misinterpretation by certain Greek translators over the years. Still, these issues are only being brought up, not so much as to encourage people towards being more erotic, or to say that women are not allowed to be celibate, or again, to say that we godbody do, or even should, force our female members to give it up more. The issue is being brought up mainly because – though marriage may be generally rejected within the godbody movement, eroticism and romance are not – eroticism, far from being condemned by Allah, was always, in actual fact, the very seal of fidelity to Allah. Indeed, the very first commandment he gave to humanity in the beginning was "Be fruitful, and multiply" (Genesis 1: 28).

Most people have been bought up with a view that romance is carnal and unspiritual, that eroticism is even profane and vulgar, but what the Song reveals, and Genesis confirms, is that eroticism plays a much more vital role in Allah's plan than has so far been presumed. That is not to say that other interpretations of the seal do not exist. Ephesians 1: 13, 14 says: "In whom ye also trusted, after that ye heard the word of truth, the gospel of your salvation: in whom also after that ye believed, ye were sealed with that holy Spirit of promise, Which is the earnest of our inheritance, until the redemption of the purchased possession, unto the praise of his glory." So, the seal could simply be a reference to the holy Spirit: thereby making what was said later in (14: 4) a lot clearer, especially as it is written there concerning those with the seal of Allah on their foreheads, "These are they which were not defiled with women; for they are virgins. These are they which follow the Lamb whithersoever he goeth. These were redeemed from among men, being the firstfruits unto God and to the Lamb."

The seal of Allah, thus, apparently, being the seal of the Holy Spirit, appears here to have no connection to the seal of passion, let alone of eroticism, spoken of in the Song of Songs; but given a closer inspection the two actually do coincide. The apostle Paul wrote for the messianic communities of Corinth, "Would to God you could bear with me a little in my folly: and indeed bear with me. For I am jealous over you with godly jealousy: for I have espoused you to one husband, that I may present you as a chaste virgin to Christ. But I fear, lest by any means, as the serpent beguiled Eve through his subtilty, so your minds should be corrupted from the simplicity that is in Christ. For if he that cometh preacheth another Jesus, whom we have not preached, or if ye receive another spirit, which ye have not received, or another gospel, which ye have not accepted, ye might well bear with him." When it said in Revelation that those sealed were virgins, it was most likely speaking in this symbolic sense, as in having no other Jesus or Spirit to corrupt them. But in that sense, the holy Spirit alone could hardly be the seal of Allah, as the holiness spoken of there is undefined. What represents the *true* holy Spirit if there are false ones that are able to beguile us?

First of all, I am not suggesting that the true Holy Spirit is erotic as such; however, the seal – which was strong as death – does appear to be such. For there is a distinction between eroticism and lust: the central difference being refinement. Thereby, even a counter-cultural articulation like hypereroticism could be appreciated as holy through the subterranean artistry of transfigured deviation. It also effectively refines *all* forms of erotic act-species, such as the wearing of transparent *djellabas* and abayas, as practices performed to demonstrate holiness. Herein can also be identified the significance of the Hebrew word *qodesh*, as it originally delineated both a classy and a sexy definition for the concept of holiness, even as such would have been understood during the days of the early messianic movement.

Even Frantz Fanon expressed – with regard to his endorsement of the appropriation or re-appropriation of identifiable traditional markers – that such practices be encouraged as forms of anti-colonial resistance, saying, "In the Arab Maghreb, the veil belongs to the clothing traditions of [the women of] the Tunisian, Algerian, Moroccan and Libyan national societies. … In the case of the Algerian man, on the other hand, regional modifications can be noted: the *fez* in urban centres, turbans and *djellabas* in the countryside" (Fanon 2006: 100). Ultimately, wearing the type of clothing that was traditional to the early messianic movement, particularly the type that we in our day would call hypererotic, distinguishes for us, demonstrably, the holy from the unholy, the clean from the unclean.

Nevertheless, for those who feel that such a definition is far too simplistic for the Most High Allah to recognise, I will proceed to remind you of the covenant that Allah made with Abraham of circumcision, the covenant Allah made with the Baptist of water baptism, and the covenant Allah made with the Prophet of the hijab. The covenants of Allah all have an element of bodily counter-cultural performance. Indeed, within Allah's requirements there is always an enactment of body-politics, a performance of corporeal flesh, that thereby signifies refinement and distinction.

Accordingly, the Holy Spirit of the first century was most likely considered nothing more than a manifestation of erotic class and refinement; and definitely not an inhibitor or disorganiser of words and behaviours. Our self-expression thereby should be a manifestation of our own divinity, as it is based on a classy and sexy spirit, and not a possessed or possessing spirit. In this manifestation it abolishes and destroys all pre-conceived ideas, thoughts, and notions, and impresses itself upon our sexuality. Thus, also actively removing any mental inhibitives and bodily performatives based on the acculturating of ourselves to our surrounding environment. In our day, it would be that which demodernises our mind and body through the acceptance of hypererotic and hypermartial honourability.

At the same time, all this has not been an entirely honest account: when (14: 4) spoke of the seal on the forehead of the hundred and forty-four thousand, what it actually said was that Allah's name was written on their foreheads. Basically, it was supposed to be Allah's very signature: and Allah's signature historically has always been some kind of demonstration of power. So, the actual question should now be: what was the significance of the forehead with regards to the seal of Allah? The only apparent answer could be that this is the location of our third eye. The signature of Allah was thus always to be the opening of our third eye, thereby allowing for us the ability to see into the astral plane at will. This truth is hereby apparent in that the Lamb that walked with them had seven eyes. Still, like with all signatures there is always a double signing. The godly sign up with hypererotic classiness (and possibly also with the practice of what I call light exhibitionism, the refusal to wear underwear), and Allah himself signs back with the opening of their third eye.

But herein can also be seen – after that the godly, both male and female, have signed themselves up to this classy and sexy lifestyle, and Allah has signed back by giving them astral vision and other supersensory abilities – that things really start to get heavy as the world now prepares to meet Allah himself at the Day of Judgment. It may therefore be asked at this point: what could those abominations possibly have been that would drive anybody to sign up to adopting a hypererotic seal like light exhibitionism in the first place even if they are classy? In order to answer this question, we must first try to remember that this sixth seal of the book of Allah, as well as the four preceding, also represented both the sixth trumpet and the sixth vial of the wine of the wrath of Allah. Whereby, to gain a better understanding of the sixth seal, particularly in its relation to the sixth vial, we will now consider what happened later on, with the outpouring of the sixth vial.

The apostle John said concerning the pouring out of the sixth vial, which represented the wine of the wrath of Allah, "And the sixth angel poured out his vial upon the great river Euphrates; and the water thereof was dried up, that the way of the kings of the east might be prepared. And I saw three unclean spirits like frogs come out of the mouth of the dragon, and out of the mouth of the beast, and out of the mouth of the false prophet. For they are the spirits of devils, working miracles, which go forth unto the kings of the earth and of the whole world, to gather them to the battle of that great day of God Almighty" (16: 12-14). The imagery painted in this is extremely clear, the warfare that has been looming throughout the course of the epistle is finally ready to transpire.

At this point, Allah prepares the way for the "kings of the east," but who are these mysterious kings of the east? To provide a level of clarity I will now say, the Latin word Orient, in its original definition, meant both rising (as in "of the sun") and the east. How this Scripture would therefore have been read in the Vulgate (Latin Bible), was, "the kings of the Orient." Again, when most of us nowadays think of the Orient we tend to think of China, Japan, Korea, and the Far East. However, this is very unlikely how the early messianic communities — especially considering that it was the Euphrates River that dried up, a river that is nowhere near modern China, Japan, or the Far East — would have interpreted it or would have been meant to interpret it. Remember, the Euphrates is in Babylon in modern-day Iraq, therefore, when the Revelation here said, "the kings of the east," or "the kings of the Orient," the most likely meaning the apostle John intended was the kings of the Near East.

It is also clear at this point that these kings were not intended to be of any royalty, nobility, or aristocracy; the issue at stake was with the wielding of political power. Therefore, we see that it was believed within the early messianic movement that an alliance of Oriental governments, which in our time would most definitely be Islamic governments, will be set and prepared on the one side. At the same time, on the other side, based on what the Scriptures just pointed out, the unclean spirits of the dragon, the Beast, and the false prophet will go out to "the kings of the earth and of the whole world." Herein, we should now be able to see that in this great warfare it will be a case of the Islamic governments, on one side, and the governments under the power of the empire of Gog and Magog, on the other side, when "he gathered them together into a place called in the Hebrew tongue Armageddon" (16: 16).

At this point you should already understand: the governments of the earth (the geo) and of the whole world (the cosmos) being under the power of the Great Empire, were always destined to go to war with the Islamic nations of Allah. Effectively, the West has been fated to go to war with Islam and their rivalry against Islam has been of long standing. Though, historically, there have been great Crusades, several of them; this particular Crusade predicted here was always set to be something different. This Crusade was to be after the time of the Great *Dajjal*. In this case, geographical and geopolitical forces will be driven by the cosmic and cosmological forces of the Dragon, the Beast, and the false prophet, to gather together against the so-called Orientals, to engage in warfare with very Allah in a place in Israel called Tel Megiddon. Tel Megiddon is a geographical area located in the valley of Jezreel where the kings of Israel historically built their palaces. The War of Tel Megiddon, at least in the minds of the children of Israel and Judea, was supposed to be a demonstration to the world of the wrath of Allah: when Allah would judge the nations of the world, those led by Gog and Magog, by the hand of Israel and Judea.

Particularly, if we consider post-exilic theory, the Judeans understood that the armies of the world would all be gathered to do battle against Allah and against his people. They believed, effectively, that, "In that day shall the Lord defend the inhabitants of Jerusalem; and he that is feeble among them at that day shall be as David; and the house of David shall be as God, as the angel of the Lord before them. And it shall come to pass in that day, that I will seek to destroy all the nations that come against Jerusalem. And I will pour upon the house of David, and upon the inhabitants of Jerusalem, the spirit of grace and of supplication: and they shall look upon me whom they have pierced, and they shall mourn for him, as one mournest for his only son, and shall be in bitterness for him, as one that is in bitterness for his firstborn. In that day shall there be a great mourning in Jerusalem, as the mourning of Hadadrimmon in the valley of Megiddon."

So, what is so significant about this valley of Megiddon? In order to fully understand its significance, one must know its biblical history. It was written in the Bible, "And Elisha the prophet called one of the children of the prophets and said unto him, Gird up thy loins, and take this box of oil in thine hand, and go to Ramoth-gilead: And when thou comest thither, look out there Jehu the son of Jehoshaphat the son of Nimishi, and go in, and make him arise up from among his brethren, and carry him to an inner chamber; Then take the box of oil, and pour it on his head, and say, Thus saith the Lord, I have anointed thee king over Israel. Then open the door, and flee, and tarry not." The reason this young prophet the prophet Elisha was sending had to immediately flee after sharing this message was that in a technical sense it could have been used against him to say that he was a conspirator and an instigator of treason, which was then, and still is in some places, a capital offence.

Now when the young prophet found Jehu he was sitting among the captains of the army, he himself being a commander among them, so the young prophet took him into a secret place and did as the prophet Elisha told him to do. When Jehu returned to the captains and told them what the young prophet had said, they immediately bowed down, then they gathered all their troops in preparation for a coup against the house of Ahab. Not too long after storming Samaria, killing the then King Joram of Israel and the then King Ahaziah of Judea, they sent word to Jezebel's servants and eunuchs that if they threw Jezebel down from her place they would be spared their lives. Sure enough, they did exactly what they said, and Queen Jezebel died instantly. Having thus taken over the royal palace, which, as noted, was in the valley of Jezreel, Jehu sent letters to the rest of the house of Ahab: seventy princes that also lived in Samaria, giving them all an opportunity to gather their forces and take back the palace. When they all openly surrendered, Jehu effectively named himself King of Israel and thus founded the Nimishi Dynasty.

One of the first things King Jehu did was then proclaim a celebration for his great victory, even as the event is recounted in the IV Book of Kings, "And Jehu said, Proclaim a solemn assembly for Baal. And they proclaimed it. And Jehu sent through all Israel: and all the worshippers of Baal came, so that there was not a man left that came not. And they came into the house of Baal; and the house of Baal was full from one end to another. And he said unto him that was over the vestry, Bring forth vestments for all the worshippers of Baal. And he brought them forth vestments. And Jehu went, and Jehonadab the son of Rechab, into the house of Baal, and said unto the worshippers of Baal, Search, and look that there be here with you none of the servants of the Lord, but the worshippers of Baal only. And when they went in to offer sacrifices and burnt offerings, Jehu appointed fourscore men without, and said, If any of the men whom I have brought into your hands escape, he that letteth him go, his life shall be for the life of him."

So that day King Jehu massacred all worshippers of Baal that came to the temple of Baal in Jezreel to worship, he also destroyed all the images of Baal and all his statues. For doing this Allah promised Jehu that his dynasty would be established, however, he also told him that for the genocide by which he destroyed them, his dynasty would only last for four generations. Herein, it came to pass that when the fourth generation finally arrived the word of Allah came to the prophet Hosea telling him to marry a promiscuous woman – possibly even a prostitute – by the name of Gomer, "So he went and took Gomer the daughter of Diblaim; which conceived, and bare him a son. And the Lord said unto him, Call his name Jezreel; for yet a little while, and I will avenge the blood of Jezreel upon the house of Jehu, and will cause to cease the kingdom of the house of Israel. And it shall come to pass at that day, that I will break the bow of Israel in the valley of Jezreel" (Hosea 1: 3-5).

To be sure, this historic event has already transpired, way back in 722 BCE with the fall of Samaria, when the Neo-Assyrian Empire officially colonised the Northern Kingdom of Israel. However, that was never intended to be the end of the matter, as the prophet Hosea said later on, "Then shall the children of Judah and the children of Israel be gathered together, and appoint themselves one head, and they shall come up out of the land: for great shall be the day of Jezreel." This was clearly an event that the prophet Ezekiel further confirmed when he said, "And I will set up one shepherd over them, and he shall feed them, even my servant David; he shall feed them, and he shall be their shepherd. And I the Lord will be their God, and my servant David a prince among them; I the Lord have spoken it. And I will make with them a covenant of peace, and will cause the evil beasts to cease out of the land: and they shall dwell safely in the wilderness, and sleep in the woods."

Consequently, just as the prophet Jeremiah prophesied a New Testament, even so the prophet Ezekiel was here prophesying a Testament of peace (or of *Islam*); reassuring those who came after that it would be David who would bring this testament of Islam to us. What can hopefully be discerned therefore is that the War of Tel Megiddon was expected to be different from what most people today have theorised. It is, in fact, most likely to be a war between the anarcho-Islamists and the Christo-fascists, due to the unclean spirits of false prophets, each working signs – which could themselves be supersensory marvels – to inspire them to go out into warfare with the people of Allah and very Allah himself. But what did the Messiah have to say about these events, "Behold, I come as a thief. Blessed is he that watcheth, and keepeth his garments, lest he walk naked, and they see his shame" (16: 15). All of which sounding pretty simple enough, but the wording is actually a gross mistranslation.

In order to give this Scripture a more perfect – or at least a more accurate and true to context – translation, I shall here translate each word of the second sentence, one by one: Blessed (*makarios*: which can translate to beautiful, happy, blessed, great, wonderful, or beatific). Is (*esti*: which can translate to is, are, or be). He (*autos*: which can translate to self, he, she, him, her, us, or they). Watcheth (*gregoreuo*: which can translate to aware, awake, woke, or vigilant). And (*kai*: which can translate to and, but, though, if, that, then, so, or too). Keepeth (*tereo*: which can translate to guard, delimit, prevent, or prohibit). His (*hautou*: which can translate to self, his, her, our, their, or them). Garments (*himation*: which can translate to apparel, fashion, clothes, clothing, or covering). Lest is not in the original texts but was most likely added or edited in to give a level of coherence to their corrupted translation. They (*autos*: which can translate to self, he, she, him, her, us, or they). Walk (*peripateo*: which can translate to live, follow, walk, or go about). Naked (*gymnos*: which can translate to train, exercise, practice, course, or naked). And (*kai*: which can translate to and, but, though, if, that, then, so, or too). They (*autos*: which can translate to self, he, she, him, her, us, or they). See (*blepo*: which can translate to gaze (upon), look (upon), perceive, or regard). His (*hautou*: which can translate to self, his, her, our, their, or them). Shame (*aschemosyne*: which can translate to indecency, immodesty, improperness, impropriety, or inelegance).

Based on these more honest word translations we can hopefully develop far more accurate sentence translations of the words spoken by the Messiah. For example: "Great are the self-aware that keep self-covered, they follow the practices and self-perceive their indecency." Or "Beautiful are they and Woke, who prohibit haute fashion; they live naked, though some gaze at their immodesty." Or "Wonderful is the Self, the vigilant one that guards; the Self, a covering, the Self, alive and naked; though the Self looks upon our inelegance." Or, finally, "Blessed be they, the awakened, that delimit their clothing when they follow this course, for they look so haute, (never) improper."

Though any one of these could make for a more contextually strong translation, suiting more accurately the actual context of early messianic practices, I suppose if I had to choose an even more precise translation for this particular text, one that would also prepare its readers to be sealed with a sexy and classy holiness, I would probably combine a few of them together to produce: "Beautiful are the self-aware that delimit their clothing: they go about naked, though some gaze at their immodesty." Why I say that this makes for a more precise translation is that the apostle John (whose surname was Marcus; see Act 12: 12 and John 19: 26, 27), was clearly, at one time, the author of Revelation, and obviously also, clearly, the most likely author of the gospel of Mark.

Accordingly, however, it is in this gospel that he included a story that may seem out of place if read inappropriately, "And there followed him a certain young man, having a linen cloth cast about his naked body; and the young men laid hold on him: And he left the linen cloth, and fled naked" (Mark 14: 51, 52). What was the purpose of adding this anecdote to his narrative about the Messiah's arrest? The best possible reasons could be, firstly, to reveal the clothing tradition of the early messianic movement: that some of them wore very Afro-chic clothing, such that would wrap-around their naked bodies. Secondly, to reveal the very truth that they were naked underneath such Afro-chic clothing (that is, that they were what I have spoken of as light exhibitionists). Thirdly, as a form of personal testimony, as who else could have possibly known the details of such an obscure story but the very author himself?

Nevertheless, at the same time, we could obviously also say with Littlewood, "A nude man and a nude woman embody [two] rather different images. The man without clothes carries a heightened sexual potential, almost a threat of rape. At the same time [this] nudity partakes of nakedness, 'stripped for action', a prosaic extension of his conventional working role. If the naked man is a self-determining subject, the undressed woman becomes an object, for men. ... [Yet, despite this truth, the] nudity of the female Earth People directly challenges this notion; like the men, they aim at being naked for themselves" (Littlewood 2006: 172) and it is here that my vision of the armed and martially trained Goddess begins to fully take shape.

Here, through the practices of light exhibitionism, sexual train running, and free love, the Black Goddess ultimately attains to a total and absolute independence from men, and even from what I call the Victorian monogamous patriarchal standard. Moreover, anarchist Malatesta made the very interesting point about this free love, "Do you think that enslaved love could really exist? Forced cohabitation exists, as does feigned and forced love, for reasons of interest or of social convenience; probably there will be men and women who will respect the bond of matrimony because of religious or moral convictions; but true love cannot exist, [or] be conceived, if it is not perfectly free." Effectively, any choice a Goddess makes to be with a man, or with men in general, should essentially be a decision she makes free from any coercive factors: whether they be those coming from societal pressures to be married and have children; or those coming from the implicit threat of some form of male dogmatic, domestic, economic, or sexual abuse.

In all, what will most likely be the real War of Tel Megiddon? It will most likely be a warfare between the anarcho-Islamists and the Christo-fascists over oppression of the worst kind. The Christo-fascists are at current the Baal worshippers idolising a false god in the form of Jesus Christ. The anarcho-Islamists, on the other hand, coming with the message of the thearchy of Allah, who exists as al-Muhibb (the Libidinal) will manifest their God through the acts of seductionism, militarism, and light exhibitionism. Herein, the war itself is over who will be God to the people: will it be Jesus Christ or Allah. To the Christo-fascists it will and must be Jesus but to the anarcho-Islamists the only God is Allah and the Messiah was only his messenger. Therein we can see that the Christo-fascists have only been vexing themselves, destroying themselves, subjugating themselves, and handing over control of the earth and of the whole world to the uninhibited powers of Gog and Magog. Accordingly, whereas the dominant empire previously had to deal with the wrath of the Lamb, now they are about to experience at full strength the inviolable wrath of very Allah himself.

Judgment Day as Declared by the Prophets

When the Lamb opened the seventh seal (8: 1-5) silence gripped the heavens for about a half an hour. This prolonged silence was not one of worship or duty but one of intensity. And then it was unleashed: the wrath of Allah longly waited for fell upon the earth to try the hearts of all Allah's enemies. Here they were now standing face to face with their greatest fear and their greatest judge, themselves. The uncleanness and injustice of their ways had been hidden from all creation, and nothing on earth knows a person like they know themselves. As they were now able to see themselves in all their filthiness, all their vanity, all their corruption, all their weakness, and all they had caused to happen within the world; if they could look on and still see the good behind the veil of Death, then, when their destiny to an eternity with likeminded individuals is fully understood, they will actually praise Allah for the final outcome.

However, for those who see failure, misery, shame, and disappointment; that see ruin, sin, and a wasted life and devotion. For them there will be horror, plague, and the unending feeling that when Allah destines them to an eternity of likeminded individuals they are and will effectively be missing out on the fulness of Allah's capacity. Moreover, for such individuals there will also be the understanding that suffering and plague will never come to an end; that they, indeed, are eternal. In this case, even the future they had believed they were striving for had always been a misreading; so that now, surrounded by likeminded, and therefore also jealous and unfulfilled people, or murderous and oppressive people they fully understand the wrath of Allah. When all the voices, and the terrors, and the thunderings, lightnings, and earthquakes have come to pass on earth, and there is nothing left on earth to stand on that cannot be shaken, it is in that moment that we must run to He who cannot be shaken, and running to him we know that he sees us and has always seen us as we truly are.

In the day that the baby bird is about to take to its first flight it calls out to, and can call out to, none other than he who is the Most High Allah. When the war-horse or chariot charges into battle, there is only one who it prays to for victory. When the rain-clouds gather, and the storms brew, there is only one whose command they await. When the rivers rush toward an aggressive coast, or are parched for lack of supply, there is only one who they depend on for strength and support. When the strong winds threaten to rip the tree from its place, or to dash the rocks and mountains with a mighty blast, only one gives them comfort and eases their fears. When the mountain lion is hungry, and becomes famished from the hunt, she stretches out her hand to no lower being. When the mountain goat is pregnant on the hills, and in pain to be delivered, she cries out to no lesser power for the deliverance of her kids. When the crocodile storms through the swamps, and takes his seat in the cloudy marsh, there is only one whom he fears, and only one to whom he does obeisance. When Shaitan is lifted up in victory, and in pride of his mighty haul, there is only one who makes him tremble, and only one who makes him submit.

In the final analysis, when humanity is through with all its fighting, and all its arrogance, and all its vanities, they too will have to stand, alone, before his judgment seat; and they too will have to give an account to none other than Allah, the Beneficent, the Merciful, the Ruler at the Day of Judgment, the Lord of all the Worlds. Yet for those who remain unconvinced, assuming that this is all just a Islamisation of biblical or Christian ideas, just remember that Islam itself was the Prophet Muhammad's attempt to, first of all, remove the various vain superstitions from the culture of his people. Second, to decolonise the minds and bodies of his people from the influence and fear of the various imperial powers surrounding Arabia. Third, and most importantly, to restore to his people a connection to their Abrahamic heritage, which may at that time have been forgotten or lost due to centuries of superstitions, on the one hand, and centuries of Falashic and Imperial Christian influence, on the other.

Essentially, the Islamic movement the Prophet Muhammad led and instigated was supposed to be a Christian movement that had always been inspired by Allah, again, with the central intent to restore the authentic Abrahamic culture. True indeed, anyone who actually, genuinely does their research will find that the proper Semitic/Falashic name for God given to Abraham in the beginning was actually the name: Allah. Moreover, the proper Hebrew name for God given in the Masoretic Bible (the supposedly authentic Bible) was never properly Elohim. Elohim in the Hebrew language is a plural for God, as in, gods. But even if we now say, alright, maybe a correct translation or transliteration is Elah, again, we find clearly a distortion. The truth is, the proper name of the God of the Hebrew Bible was always, and has always been, Allah. Furthermore, during the days of the New Testament: when the Baptist and the Messiah spoke to the people, the then common language was neither Hebrew nor Greek. The common language in the Israel and Judea of their time was Aramaic, which is another Semitic language. Now Aramaic is also a language still spoken in Palestine to this day by various Palestinian Christians, and what is the name they, in Aramaic, use for God? Again, it is Allah.

Allah is and has always been the name of the Hebrew God from the time of Abraham to the time of the Prophet Muhammad. Muhammad did not make the name up, or develop it by combining this concept with that idea. If anyone made up the name it would have been Abraham, yet even this is questionable. The fact is, Allah is the name of the God of the Hebrew tradition, as noted, from the time of Abraham to the time of Muhammad; a truth that actually gives newer and greater meaning to a Scripture heavily, and intentionally, misinterpreted within Christianity: "And I will pour upon the house of David, and upon the inhabitants of Jerusalem, the spirit of grace and of supplication: and they shall look upon *me* whom they have pierced, and they shall mourn for him, as one mournest for his only son, and shall be in bitterness for him, as one that is in bitterness for his firstborn. In that day shall there be a great mourning in Jerusalem, as the mourning of Hadadrimmon in the valley of Megiddon" (Zechariah 12: 10, 11; emphasis mine).

The one Allah had prophesied that was supposed to be pierced was never meant to be the Messiah, though the apostle John purposely led his followers to believe that. It was not that the apostle John lied, or was even purposefully trying to deceive, but that the original message of the Messiah was always one leading to Allah, in which the God of the Messiah, again, in Aramaic: Allah, was the true and rightful king of his announced thearchy. Even the Prophet had written in these Quranic verses, saying, "The Messiah disdains not to be a servant of Allah, nor do the angels who are sent to Him. And whoever disdains His service and is proud, He will gather them all together to Himself. Then as for those who believe and do good, He will pay them fully their rewards and give them more out of His grace. And as for those who disdain and are proud, He will chastise them with a painful chastisement, and they will find for themselves besides Allah no friend nor helper" (Quran 4: 172, 173).

The apostle Paul further stated along these lines, "Now this I say, brethren, that flesh and blood cannot inherit the kingdom of God; neither doth corruption inherit incorruption." Thereby revealing that the kingdom of God (or, again, in our own case, Black thearchism), is not for the corporeal, nor is it itself corporeal. Indeed, the Divine Parousia of the Messiah may not even in itself be a corporeal Parousia. It may in fact of necessity be an astral Parousia. A lot of believers, nowadays, love to say how the Messiah will fix all the world's problems at his Second Parousia, when Allah has already given us the means to fix everything that needs fixing right now thanks to the First Parousia. Further, as was also said concerning the Second Parousia: "the Lord himself shall descend from heaven with a shout, with the voice of the archangel, and with the trump of God: and the dead in Christ shall rise first: Then we which are alive and remain shall be caught up together with them in the clouds, to meet the Lord in the air: and so shall we ever be with the Lord" (1Thessalonians 4: 16, 17).

Now the apostle Paul had already said that flesh and blood do not inherit the kingdom of God, also the word he used here for "air" is the word *pneuma* which can also translate to spirit, so this was clearly not considered by him to be a corporeal resurrection. Considering these things a little more thoroughly perhaps the best way to answer this Scriptural question is by going deeper into further Scriptures. The apostle John provided us with an answer to the riddle that has far more depth and weight to it, "After this I looked, and behold, a door was opened in heaven: and the first voice which I heard was as it were of a trumpet talking with me; which said, Come up hither, and I will shew thee things which must be hereafter. And immediately I was in the spirit: and behold, a throne was set in heaven, and one sat on the throne. And he that sat was to look upon like a jasper and a sardine stone: and there was a rainbow round about the throne in sight like unto an emerald. And round about the throne were four and twenty seats: and upon the seats I saw four and twenty elders sitting, clothed in white raiment" (4: 1-5). All this was an experience the apostle John recounted of his own enrapturement, of the hereafter, and of heavenly bliss, yet all entirely *astral* in manifestation, as everything that happened took place while he happened to be "in the spirit," that is in the *pneuma*.

At the same time, this biblical Scripture also presents us with a completely uncommon description of the Ancient of Days and his divine ones from the current White images shown around the world today (seeing that jasper is in fact a reddish brown colour very similar to mahogany and sardius is in fact an orangey brown colour in sight very similar to varnished oak). The picture the apostle John seems to have painted here was thereby a picture of Black deities. So now, how do we make sense of this reality? Jose Malcioln becomes most helpful in this instant, especially in his expressing this statement that our ancestors, "The Cushites, [the] fathers of all … black people … [were] celebrated Cushite kings [and were] usually deified after death, and sometimes metamorphosed to be identified with the stars and constellations". Moreover, as he would further continue, "the Greeks often visited Africa when she abounded in glory, and referred to the Cushites [themselves] as gods."

So, what is the godbody outlook of the Divine Parousia? To us it comes though Black people understanding the interconnection between the Black race, divinity, nobility, Africa, and theocentrism. Conversely, according to Boyce Rensenberger, "Evidence of the oldest recognizable monarchy in human history, preceding the rise of the earliest Egyptian Kings by several generations, has been discovered in artifacts from ancient Nubia in Africa." These Nubian people being highly civilised, classy, wise, and beautiful, were also excessively adventurous. Yet, as Malcioln stated again, "Once the Nubians traveled to other lands wearing as much gold jewelry as they did, people of paler skin began to visit Cush to trade." Thus giving us an idea of the wonder and impression these ancestors of ours must have had on those people outside of Africa. Indeed, the Parousia of the Gods and Goddesses of our time may not even be able to capture the realities of what our ancestors were really like in those times.

Malcioln further explained the aftereffects of the ancient interactions with these Nubian gods and goddesses, and in particular the Divine Goddesses, saying, "An unusual sight was the Nubian woman in her splendor and beauty. She was beautiful to admire as she approached, irresistible to behold when she passed and gracefully displayed her protruding buttocks. The Nubian woman did not require a crinoline petticoat or hoop-skirt with a wire cage to attract a man of good taste. And when the foreigners discovered that it was not necessary to put a pillow under her to obtain the peristaltic movements so gratifying in harmonious sexual relations, they sought her favors or took her by force."

To understand better the realities of what transpired during this process of Nubian (or ancient Ethiopian) development Malcioln continued, "As a result [of the violent and non-violent sexualisation of the Nubian woman], there are [now] fifty or more tribal groups with separate customs and looks. There are also about fifty languages spoken, and four times as many dialects." Consequently, "The original language group of Ethiopia was Cushitic. It was not until the first millenium B.C.E. that the Semitic people, called Habasat, entered Ethiopia from southern Arabia. ... [Ultimately], the Semitic-Ethiopic languages became Ge'ez, Tigre, Tigrina, Amharic, Argoba, Harari, Gurage, and Gufat." From these beginnings came the Kushite/Nubian people, who were the true fathers and mothers of civilisation, and the first true and living Gods and Goddesses of the planet.

Now, any neighbourhood that thereby accepts this reality will also thereby experience, at that moment, the Divine Parousia, and from that moment begin to dwell in the body of God.

It is now, therefore, the declared intention of Black style godbodyism to overthrow all the existing forces of American style liberalism, and thereby to replace the existing rule of law with the literal rule of Allah. To be sure, liberalism will never willing lie down to godbodyism, it will therefore have to be overcome and overthrown. But this overthrowing need not involve terrorism or even coercion. The mature system (if it is really the desire of the people to call it that) is based on socially and theologically ethical people living to manifest their own divinity. This is not the liberalistic "rule of law," amounting to nothing really but the rule of the bourgeoisie; this is the thearchic rule of libido, effectively amounting to the rule of Allah.

Basically, the Day of Allah was to come after the Lamb had judged the nations of the world, led by Gog and Magog, by the hand of his once dispersed, and even now still dispersed, people of Israel in warfare. This Day of Allah, being therefore preceded by the Second Parousia of the Messiah, should not be considered interchangeable with it. At the same time, to the godbody the Divine Parousia is itself in accordance with Black individuals realising in their hearts that they and their ancestors are, and have always been, the true Gods and Goddesses of the planet earth. From that moment on they essentially will dwell in an actually existing millenarianism of poor righteous teachers of Black divinity. Still, the potential of this thearchy coming into the neighbourhoods of the world have already likely caused the rulers and governments of the earth and of the whole world, led by the empire of Gog and Magog, to prepare their own fight back in the form of an Armageddon War.

It is for this cause that Allah, again, said through his prophet Joel that there are, "Multitudes, multitudes in the valley of decision: for the day of the Lord is near in the valley of decision." If, indeed, this valley of decision was always intended to be nothing more than an allusion to the valley of Tel Megiddon, then we see that the decision to be made was, and has always been, the most ultimate decision. Will you allow Allah to overthrow all the false teachings and false deities in your heart, and thus accept the divinity of your own self and kind? If you choose the affirmative then, and only then, will come afterwards an individually experienced tribulation.

Nevertheless, the apostle Paul had this to say on the matter: "we must through much tribulation enter into the kingdom of God" (Acts 14: 22). The individually experienced tribulation they go through will obviously come as a result of state sponsored persecution, a persecution they endure because of the revelation they received of the Messiah in the *pneuma*. However, the Armageddon War comes when those persecuted during this Great Tribulation make the revolutionary decision to fight back against their persecutors, and it is only at that point that the people of Allah will need to employ the help of the God you now.

The Epistle of Revelation in Godbody Eschatology

Though we godbodies all claim cultural Islam, thereby practicing the *culture* of Islam, many of us look to inspiration from the Bible, and particularly from the epistle of Revelation. Indeed, the epistle of Revelation has legendary status for us among the other books of the Bible. Written most likely by the apostle John Marcus (Acts 15: 37) it contains very eschatological imagery. Although a large number of Christians, since the time of Eusebius of Caesarea, have connected the Revelation to a an Elder John, Lizokin-Eyzenberg and Shir explained that the evidence for the authorship of the Revelation being by the apostle John is actually stronger than that of the Gospel of John, which was most likely written by a scribe skilled in Greek letters. The unlettered Judean apostle of first century Galilee obviously wrote the Revelation like any child of the ghetto writing in the traditional Judean apocalyptic style; using Greek to the best of his still relatively unlearned abilities. Regardless, the apostolic authorship of Revelation is the direction this book has taken.

In the Revelation John introduced three mythic characters, like any Greek comedy introducing its main villains: First, the Dragon, who is "called the Devil, and Satan, which deceiveth the whole world" (12: 9). This character is introduced as the primary villain, the one who opposes the hero, who is the Messiah. Second, the Beast, who ascended out of the bottomless pit, and goes into perdition. This Beast is called "in the Hebrew tongue … Abaddon, but in the Greek tongue hath his name Apollyon" (9: 11). Third, Babylon the Great, who is "THE MOTHER OF HARLOTS AND ABOMINATIONS OF THE EARTH" (17: 5). Further, according to the apostle John, the Beast "shall hate the whore, and shall make her desolate and naked, and shall eat her flesh, and burn her with fire" (17: 16). Basically, the house of the villains is already a house divided against itself; this is what allows what would otherwise have been a tragedy to become a comedy.

However, it is not the hope or even the comedy aspect of the Revelation that the godbody adopted within its own eschatology, it is the language of Revelation that is more valuable to us than the visionary elements. Within the 1-10 of the godbody 120 lessons it is asked, "Who is the colored man? The colored man is the Caucasian White man, Yaqub's grafted devil of the planet earth." This answer is open to misinterpretation. Many have taken it to mean that we godbody see White people as evil and wicked because we see them as devils grafted by Yaqub. That is not the case. We see White supremacy as evil and wicked and the White people who follow White supremacy not as an absolute evil, but still as evil, yet mainly for that reason, as such, and not for being grafted.

Indeed, many White people take serious issue with being called the devil. Such language they claim as racist in its own right. To those in the Black community who buy into this garbage I wish to say: the oppressor never likes being called an oppressor; the exploiter never likes being called an exploiter; the victimiser never likes being called a victimiser; the abuser never likes being called an abuser; the misogynist never likes being called a misogynist; the transphobic never likes being called a transphobic, so, the devil never likes being called a devil. The truth is, power rarely sees its oppressive nature as anything unnatural or unjust; it instead sees its power as very natural and justly earned. Hereby, we see the narratives White supremacy has told itself to maintain power are based on a discourse of White superiority that justifies their right to power, their right to supremacy.

In many ways Cone shared a similar view and encouraged this perception for Black theology, however, he did not consider White people to be devils for their White supremacy. But if we consider where devilishment came from in the first place we get an understanding that what caused the devil to fall at the origin was a superiority complex: the devil felt superior to God and so fell, or the devil felt superior to Adam and so fell. Whatever way you look at it it was a superiority feeling and power imbalance that led the devil to become a devil. Well, the discourse of White superiority and the ideology of White supremacy are the current conclusions of devilishment. In other words, whether Black theology likes it or not, whether we appreciate it or not, White people will be the living devil until proven otherwise.

The godbodies take such a radical approach saying that as long as White supremacy exists in the world White people will be devils, this is because we know what oppression, exploitation, and victimisation look like, and in every case, it comes from a system created by them. The devilishment, however, is not in that the system was created by them, but that it not only heavily favours them, but undermines, oppresses, and victimises all that is other to their standards. This system also makes White people devils by giving them a heavily exalted unconscious opinion of themselves, while subjecting all other races to the threat of their social and systemic privilege being weaponised against them. Moreover, with White privilege having become unconscious through both biases and micro-aggressions being used without thought of hurt, repercussion, or public opinion, the devil, at least to us godbodies, is White people.

To us also, from among the White population comes the Anti-Christ (*al-Dajjal*), but there is also separately a Beast. Many of us view the *Dajjal* as a man, but the Beast as a system: the Great United States Empire (GUSE). To many of us the *Dajjal* shall lead the Beast to war with the Black race, but the Beast is a system not a person. There are seven heads of the Beast according to Revelation, these are not problematic as such: they possibly represent the political ideals that America stood for and stands for. The Beast being the corruption of those ideals. The apostle John said, "the beast that was, and is not, even he is the eighth, and is of the seven, and goeth into perdition." The Beast was and is not: the was part is the seven heads, the is not part is what the US empire corrupted those heads into. In that sense it never was, as America never really lived up to the ideals it proclaimed it believed in. On an even more meta level, the Beast that is not is the *Dajjal*, as he is not a head but is of the seven and "goeth into perdition."

But ultimately, to many of us, the GUSE is the Beast and the *Dajjal* rises from within the Beast as its strongest representative. Indeed, he could be called "America personified." In this sense, America is very important to the destiny of the world, as the last great empire it will play the biggest role in global events. Moreover, the Great Tribulation will feature the US persecuting Black people substantially, worse than they have persecuted us since the Civil Rights movement. At least, that was for a long time the belief of those godbodies that believed in the Great Tribulation or *Fitnah al-Akbar.*

Yet, there is another layer to the Beast being Imperial America that should be acknowledged, the belly of the Beast. In this understanding the belly of the Beast is not a country or person but the US prison-industrial complex. Just as the Beast is seen by many godbodies as the system of the GUSE, so the belly of the Beast is seen by these godbodies as the system of the prison-industrial complex. I know this because when I was locked up in prison, I heard many godbodies referring to our prison as the belly of the Beast. Here the eschatological symbolism was removed, and the language was based significantly on the so-called "now of eschatology." Again, being in the belly of any animal means being eaten. The metaphorical idea is that we were consumed and swallowed whole by the Beast (GUSE) and once vomited back onto the streets we would forever have a prison sentence tarnishing our record.

The final villain the apostle John spoke of in Revelation, that we godbody sometimes use in our language, is Babylon. In Revelation Babylon was likely either Rome or Jerusalem, however, to us Babylon is the US government and law enforcers. While many would call the police Babylon, following the Rastafarian ideas of Babylon, we would also call the FBI, DEA, SWAT, and USIB Babylon. We would even call the judges, lawyers, politicians, clergy, and professors Babylon. So, while to us the Beast is the system of the GUSE; Babylon, to many of us, is those who maintain the system, oppose street culture, and will oppose Black people as a whole during the time of the *Fitnah al-Akbar.*

As the Beast turns on Babylon so the system will turn on those who maintain it. Or to be more precise, a *dajjal* and his followers will oppose the timidity of the GUSE in its dealing with Black people, especially at the time that the Witness arises. But Babylon will fall, according to the Elijah Muhammad, and will be left without refuge. He said, "America hates the doers of good and seeks to destroy them. This is the cause of the fall of America." Moreover, he continued, "Never before America has there been a nation on the face of the earth where scores of murders take place daily and nightly. In one large metropolitan city of America, the death rate is terrific ... children kill children ... male is against male and female is against female, destroying each other."

A final terminology that the godbody use that is derived from the Revelation is the mark of the Beast. This mark, used in the Revelation to signify those belonging to the Beast and corrupted by him, indeed, those who worship the Beast and will partake of his judgment, is used by the godbody in a similar way. Those who have been influenced by the Charismatics say the mark of the Beast will be a computer chip, as that is what the Charismatics say. Those who have been influenced by the Jews say the mark of the Beast will be a Scripture or a corruption of the Scriptures (in their case, the Torah), as that is what Deuteronomy 11: 18 implies. Those who have been influenced by the anti-vac crowd say the mark of the Beast will be a vaccine, as such a reality seems very possible in our day. However, those of us who are learned know that the name *Neron Qesar* (Nero Caesar) added up to 666, which was defined by the apostle John to be the real mark of the Beast.

Based on this idea there are a small minority of us who say that the mark of the Beast is belief in the White Jesus. This is based on a second opinion about the Beast: that it is the Roman Catholic Church. That is not to say all Catholics are evil or going to hell or anything that morbid, I myself am a practicing Catholic and a cultural Muslim – similar to the Mozarabs of Spain – this is to say that the Roman Empire was never really destroyed after its fall. In the first century, when the apostle John wrote the Revelation, the Roman Empire was still very strong and had no serious signs of ever falling. Yet Rome did fall in 476 CE. At that time, all that remained of the Roman Empire was the Roman Catholic Church. But maybe that is it, the Catholic Church remained in Rome and maintained a system of clergy and church government similar to the fallen empire. In that sense, Rome never really did fall, as Catholicism remained. Then, with the return of empire in the form of the Holy Roman Empire, the Popes played a significant role in governing the masses.

However, around the time of the Renaissance something changed: around about that time the Catholics began painting Jesus as a White man. The first instances of this being during the Renaissance, it is for this cause that we consider the White Jesus to be the Beast that was, and is not, and never was. The White Jesus was created by Catholicism and has corrupted everyone it has encountered. A bold statement but one that is proven by the realities of White supremacy. White supremacy could not have existed without the White Jesus. By painting Christ as a White man, they thereby defined themselves as God-people. There is obviously an irony here in that the godbody, by definition, consider Black people to be divine people; however, we do not define God as they do. To them God is defined by power, and power has always been used to determine White supremacy. To us God is defined by intelligence, hence why always read.

Those of us who call the White Christ the Anti-Christ (*al-Dajjal*) and the Roman Catholic Church the Beast say the battle between the Beast and Babylon – which we still say is America, in this case the Great United States Empire – is more likely a battle between Religion and the State. Hence, the kingdom of the devil (White supremacy) will be divided against itself. Again, all this may be fine and well, but was this really the interpretation the apostle John had in mind when he wrote the Revelation? Indeed, the White Christ and the United States of America did not exist to the apostle John so how could he really, in all honesty, have been writing to seven historical communities in the Roman province of Asia about these realities. Moreover, how do we go about finding the true interpretations that the apostle John had in mind when he wrote the Revelation? Who did the apostle John consider to be the Beast and is this in any ways related to what we godbody teach or have taught?

To find the apostle John's ideas of the Beast and his mark we must first go to (13: 18) where it says, "Here is wisdom. Let him that hath understanding count the number of the beast: for it is the number of a man; and his number is Six hundred threescore and six [666]". This is not the only time wisdom (*sophia*) is mentioned in relation to the Beast. As it said later on, "And here is the mind which hath wisdom. The seven heads are seven mountains, on which the woman sitteth. And there are seven kings: five are fallen, and one is, and the other is not yet come; and when he cometh, he must continue a short space".

As Lizokin-Eyzenberg and Shir (2021) noted, this can be open to a number of interpretations. Their personal interpretation is based on having seen a coin minted in the first century with an image of Emperor Vespasian on one side and an image of the goddess Roma on the other side sitting on seven hills. This evidence is compelling as the first century messianic communities would no doubt have seen this coin and would therefore be more familiar with this than they would have been with a White Christ or with the nation of America. In this sense, the seven mountains are the Seven Hills of Rome, and the seven kings could be interpreted as seven Caesars, seven marking the number of completion to first century Judeans.

However, there were actually twelve Caesars, so the "five are fallen, and one is, and the other is not yet come" quote becomes quite problematic to this interpretation. Also remember, this is for "the mind which hath wisdom," simplistic interpretations like that would therefore stumble the average reader but not the deep thinker. So, if it is not the Seven Hills of Rome and seven Caesars why is there such striking symmetry? The answer to this is found in (12: 1-5) where a woman clothed with the sun, and the moon under her feet, and a crown of twelve stars was with child and in pain at its delivery. Then a red dragon, having seven heads and ten horns stood in front of the woman to devour her child as soon as it was born. This story resembles uncannily the story of the Egyptian goddess Auset. Indeed, the cult of Auset was very popular throughout the first century Roman Empire. Yet it is unlikely he meant for the vision of 12: 1-5 to be interpreted as the story of Auset and her son Horu. Sometimes a little knowledge can be a dangerous thing.

In this case, two far more likely scenarios to have influenced the apostle John were (i) the apostle combining the Auset imagery to his relationship with the Messiah's mother: thereby imagining a dreaded women wearing a twelve point tiara; also having a pregnant body while wearing a topless, fine-spun, golden-orange, African wrapper known as a *Kaftan*; and having her own brazen orange feet standing atop a white circle. (ii) Solomon's Song of Songs where Queen Makeda of Sheba said of herself, "I am black, but comely, O ye daughters of Jerusalem, as the tents of Kedar, as the curtains of Solomon" (Song of Solomon 1: 5), and where, moreover, it was said of her,

"Who is she that looketh forth as the morning, fair as the moon, clear as the sun, and terrible as an army with banners?" (Song of Solomon 6: 10). Here, the sun-kissed Queen of Sheba represented the African queen of heaven, carrying many of the symbols used by the apostle John in his Revelation.

So, like with any modern-day rapper that uses a quadruple entendre, the apostle John hid several layers of meaning within the words he used. Not to mention the Author that masterminded the entire visionary sequence. Thereby, the mind which hath *sophia* would have known: the Bible, as a whole, speaks of six mountains that were used by six prophets – five are fallen, and one is, and the other is not yet come. The six mountains that were fallen were Mount Horeb, Mount Zion, Mount Moriah, Mount Carmel, Mount Samaria, and Mount Olivet. The six Kings were Moses, David, Solomon, Elijah, Amos, and Jesus. Based on this picture it is easy to see who the seventh head is, Muhammad, and the mountain is Mount Hirah. Furthermore, within this list there is great chiastic symmetry.

A1. Mount Horeb – Arabian Mountain
    B1. Mount Zion – Davidic Mountain
        C1. Mount Moriah – Religious Mountain
            D. Mount Carmel – Prophetic Mountain
        C2. Mount Samaria – Religious Mountain
    B2. Mount Olivet – Davidic Mountain
A2. Mount Hirah – Arabian Mountain

Herein, the head of the seven that "as it were [was] wounded to death" (13: 3) was not Jesus but Muhammad, as he is the prophet that has been excluded from all Roman Catholic doctrine and ideas.

So again, the question now becomes, was this the apostle John's intention? If you take the author of the Revelation to be the author of the Gospel of John, then something quite interesting becomes apparent. There is a story in John's Gospel that is in no other gospel, which is about a Samaritan woman at a well. In it, "Jesus saith unto her, Go call thy husband, and come hither. The woman answered and said, I have no husband. Jesus said unto her, Thou hast well said, I have no husband: For thou hast had five husbands; and he whom thou now hast is not thy husband: in that saidst thou truly" (John 4: 16-18). We can be sure of two things from this quote, firstly, John was not present when the Messiah had this conversation with the woman, secondly, it is unlikely that the Messiah ever told anybody, whether privately or publicly, what he actually did say to that woman. If that is the case, why did the apostle John say that that was what the Messiah said? To interpret to those with wisdom the mystery of the Beast.

The clue is when the woman said, "Our fathers worshipped in this mountain [Mount Samaria]; and ye say, that in Jerusalem is the place where men ought to worship." Obviously, this interpretation falls apart if the author of the Revelation was not the author of the Gospel of John, so it is up for debate. The more common interpretation of the seven mountains being the Seven Hills of Rome has higher symbolic value: in this case Babylon is Rome and the Beast is the Roman Empire. But if this book is correct then who really is Babylon? Is the Beast really the great prophets of history? And are these ideas not a stretch, even a blasphemous stretch? The answer is found, again, in Revelation, "And the beast that was, and is not, even he is the eighth, and is of the seven, and goeth into perdition." The seven heads are not evil as such; it is the corruption of them by the Beast that makes them evil. Hence, the apostle

John most likely did have in mind the corruption of the Messiah into something that he was not when he wrote about the Beast, thereby making the White Christ a very likely candidate for the Anti-Christ, the Great *Dajjal*.

The Messiah himself also finalised this point, saying, "When ye therefore shall see the abomination of desolation, spoken of by Daniel the prophet, stand in the holy place, (whoso readeth, let him understand:) Then let them which be in Judea flee into the mountain" (Matthew 24: 15, 16). The apostle Paul, however, gave an even more in depth interpretation, saying, "Let no man deceive you by any means; for that day shall not come, except there come a falling away first, and that man of sin be revealed, the son of perdition; who opposeth and exalteth himself above all that is called God, or that is worshipped; so that he as God sitteth in the temple of God, shewing himself that he is God" (Thessalonians 2: 3, 4). Clearly, when the "son of perdition" takes his seat in the temple of God telling himself that he is God that will be the abomination of desolation spoken of by the prophet Daniel.

Having said all that, let us look more closely at the actual section of the apocalypse of Daniel to see what it said and what the prophet Daniel really believed would be the fate of the Great *Dajjal*: "the ships of Chittim shall come against him: therefore he shall be grieved, and return, and have indignation against the holy covenant: so shall he do; he shall even return, and have intelligence with them that forsake the holy covenant. And arms shall stand on his part, and they shall pollute the sanctuary of strength, and shall take away the daily sacrifice, and [put in its] place the abomination that maketh desolate" (Daniel 11: 30, 31). Clearly, the sanctuary of strength is where the Great *Dajjal* sets up his abomination of desolations, so that now the question becomes: where is this "sanctuary of strength"?

Where is this "holy place," or this "temple of God"? To answer these the apostle Paul gave us a clear definition: "Know ye not that ye are the temple of God, and that the Spirit of God dwelleth in you?" (1Corinthians 3: 16). The temple, sanctuary, or holy place of Allah are not in some building in Jerusalem but in the holy people of Allah.

So now, the question is: what kinds of sacrifices will this *Dajjal* seek to put an end to? The sacrifices of praise? The tithes of finances? In theory both, but in truth neither. The *Dajjal* does not end or take away such, he merely directs them toward himself, even as it is written, "Take heed that no man deceive you. For many shall come in my name saying, I am Christ; and shall deceive many." "For if he that cometh preacheth another Jesus, whom we have not preached, or if ye receive another spirit, which ye have not received, or another gospel, which ye have not accepted, ye might well bear with him" (Matthew 24: 4, 5; 2Corinthians 11: 4). So, what is the abomination of desolations? The seating in the heart of God's people a false Jesus from the historical Jesus.

Returning again to the prophet Daniel, it says, "And the king shall do according to his will; and he shall exalt himself, and magnify himself above every god, and shall speak marvellous things against the God of gods, and shall prosper till the indignation be accomplished: for that that is determined shall be done" (Daniel 11: 36). Let me paraphrase the last part "he shall prosper until the time of the heathen be accomplished." As noted earlier: after Chittim (Hebrew code for Rome) attacks, he will abandon the holy covenant. Sounds like Protestantism to me; that is, the immediate post-Renaissance. From that time, they began to set up an abomination that has left so many nations in the world — the vast majority of the planet even — desolate. The single-eyed mission of this Great *Dajjal* to exalt himself above all that is called God or that is worshipped, and to make the people of the world bow down to his image was excessively successful. But he cheated, and Allah knows it.

Nevertheless, the question could now be asked: what about America, surely the apostle John did not have in mind a nation as yet unknown to him and his people? However, it should be clear to anyone who does a deep dive into the epistle of Revelation that the apostle John set up four Manichean dichotomies: God and the Devil, the Lamb and the Beast, the Witness and the false prophet, Jerusalem and Babylon. Based on this dualism, if Black people are symbolic of the New Jerusalem, then America must be symbolic of Babylon. Indeed, if America itself were to ever fall, then, "the kings of the earth, who have committed fornication and lived deliciously with her, shall bewail her," "And the merchants of the earth shall weep and mourn over her" (18: 9, 11).

Still, I have, again, not been entirely honest with you: though most street lifers use the language of Babylon in their discourse, most of us godbodies actually do not. We have, however, been known to use the term Magog as a surrogate for devil when talking about Caucasians. Effectively, as the historical Magog is presumed to have been located by the Caucasus Mountains, so Gog and Magog are accepted by some of us to be symbolic of Caucasian people. Herein, the empire of Babylon, the third villain in the epistle of Revelation, is not as important as the two cameoed villains at the very end, Gog and Magog, as the empire of Caucasian people. Accordingly, the White Christ is believed by some in the godbody, though admittedly, again, a minority, to be the Anti-Christ (*al-Dajjal*), Christianity (both Catholic and Protestant) to be the Beast, the Western penitentiary system to be the belly of the

Beast, images of the White Christ to be the mark of the Beast, Caucasian people as a whole to be Magog, and the American Empire more specifically to be Babylon.

But how then do we reconcile all these ideas with the picture of eschatology painted so far? We say that among the Caucasians there will probably arise a little *dajjal* who will oppose a little messiah. This little messiah will be Khidr, the Great Witness, while the little *dajjal* will be the false prophet who declares himself to be a prophet of Christianity. The one who will arise first I do not know but both will be supersensory. The false prophet will lead people toward the White Christ, the Witness toward Allah and the Blackness of Moses, Jesus, and all the apostle and prophets. The false prophet will inspire Babylon to oppress Black people; while the Witness will inspire Jerusalem to fight back against their oppressors.

When Babylon gets a whiff of the violence being used against these White oppressors the state will begin to clamp down on the Witness and on his or her followers. Now, as Babylon is symbolic of America so the Euphrates is symbolic of an American line that will eventually be crossed: the state-sponsored persecution will then become an Armageddon War and Martial Law will be put into force. Then, "the brother shall betray the brother to death, and the father the son; and children shall rise up against their parents, and shall cause them to be put to death. And ye shall be hated of all men for my name's sake" (Mark 13: 12, 13). This will be Babylon coming down hard on Black people. The Christians who are good enough will hate Babylon for persecuting us under the rubric of anti-terrorism.

Yet it will be around this time that war, famine, death, and hell will be unleashed against Babylon for all their cruelty towards our people. At the same time, the false prophet, or little *dajjal*, will probably have enough political capital to win for himself the Presidency of the Babylonian Empire. It is then that he will pass a law concerning the White Christ that will be supported by most Evangelical Americans but opposed by those inspired by the Witness. Finally, the Witness will be caught and arrested for treason. Then, at the behest of the *dajjal*, he or she will be murdered either in his or her cell or taken and brought somewhere no one else knows about to be killed.

Conclusion

In conclusion, this book has attempted to show how the godbody eschatology is a kind of Islamic eschatology, all of which are themselves eschatologies based on historicity. It has also attempted to communicate how the godbody eschatology, being an Islamic eschatology with an Islamic view of God, takes that historicity and captures the circumstances under which it can actually be applied. In sum, it has shown how the godbody eschatology relates to Islamic eschatological visions, while, at the same time, showing that godbody theory has a very definite and realistic timeline.

Moreover, this book has also attempted to prove that, "Neo-colonialism is [in fact] the worst form of imperialism. For those who practice it, it means power without responsibility and for those who suffer from it, it means exploitation without redress" (Nkrumah 2022: 3). Furthermore, the underlying premise of neo-colonialism is that culturally there is a hierarchy: even as racism is based largely on a biological hierarchy, "the cultures supposed implicitly superior are those which appreciate and promote 'individual' enterprise, social and political individualism, as against those which inhibit these things" (Balibar 1991: 25). As individualism is an Americanised concept promoted to all nations as a "universal ethic" for humanity, America undermines all the so-called "cultural maladies" of its imperial subjects in order to bring to them the "civilisation" they believe they have.

Invariably, "This latent presence of the hierarchic theme … finds its chief expression in the priority accorded to the individualistic model" (Balibar 1991: 25); thus making all opposition, whether in the West or the non-West, appear as though it is backward or at least infantile. Indeed, what is currently called globalisation is really just a ruse for neo-colonialism. Things will therefore not change until we appreciate that it is not enough to speak or write against American imperialism, we must actually fight, even with violence, against it; and whenever such a decision begins to occur, we, the once persecuted people of the world, will, from that point on, need to employ the help of the God you now.

Series Postscript

Though this series is and will be very controversial throughout, especially for one who is a self-proclaimed Black theologian. Nevertheless, considering that the Black thearchy I have herein sought to promote to the world is neither a corrupt authoritarian, nor a chaotic utopian, system, but in fact an already existing ghetto movement, our motive is not the ultimate overthrow of existing bourgeois society. All we seek is merely the defending of our actually existing culture, traditions, and doctrinal viewpoints, even as they currently stand, and not the allowing of any modernist standards or opinions to corrupt them or contaminate any of our existing doctrinal interpretations; regardless of the level of persecution we receive for carrying them.

In modern society the main and central differentiation between revolutionary deviance and criminal malevolence is a matter of internal perspective: just like "one man's terrorist is another man's freedom fighter." Distinction is also perceptible through a person's level of internal consciousness. Or to better clarify, the central disparity between a criminal and a freedom fighter *is* their level of consciousness. Yet using such a reductionist simplification one could draw the further conclusion that all that really distinguishes a freedom fighter from the divine is, in this case, their level of *habba* (libido). Here, through altering perspectives we can hopefully attain to a raising of *habba*, and thereby of divinity in the street life.

Ultimately, through strengthening the social forces of ghetto culture we can effectively begin the process of abolishing White privilege, and overthrowing this whole corrupt system of White supremacy. Herein, the godbody movement provides a wealth of guidance, and access to many lessons that may prove quite complex. For this cause, if you currently wish to learn more about our movement (I get paid nothing for this endorsement), feel free to write to the address below:

The Allah School in Mecca
2122 7th Avenue
New York, NY 10027
USA

Also be sure to let them know that it was a book in this series that inspired you to join. Once they have been informed as to your true intentions they should be willing to give you everything you need to be an enlightened part of this movement.

Lastly, I have really enjoyed writing this book; and as a part of my *Black Divinity Series* it has been a key facet and aspect of my life's work as a theologian and biblical scholar. For this cause, I currently make this final request: that if you have gained or learned anything you feel to be of value please remember to leave a review on the platform from which you purchased this book. Small things like that help authors like me gain wider readership and validation for our efforts. They also give us the opportunity to hear some of the stories of those we have touched with our work. Thank you for your support, much love and peace.

Attention African American Theologians!!!

Imagine the Beauties of Life Unfolded, the Wisdom of the Ages Revealed, and the Mysteries of God Come to Light

A Godbody Theology of the First Resurrection is the third instalment in Shahidi Islam's *Black Divinity Series*.
Based on decades of research, see many of the truths distorted by years of slavery and colonialism now uncovered. To learn more shop now.

A Godbody Theology of the First Resurrection

Bibliography

Abraham, N (1994); "Notes on the Phantom a Complement to Freud's Metapsychology." In N. T. Rand (Ed), *The Shell and the Kernel*; University of Chicago Press.

Abraham, N (1994); "The Phantom of Hamlet or The Sixth Act preceded by The Intermission of 'Truth'." In N. T. Rand (Ed), *The Shell and the Kernel*; University of Chicago Press.

Abraham, N & Torok, M (1994); "Mourning or Melancholia: Introjection Versus Incorporation." In N. T. Rand (Ed), *The Shell and the Kernel*; University of Chicago Press.

Abron, J. M (2005); "'Serving the People': The Survival Programs of The Black Panther Party." In C. E. Jones (Ed), *The Black Panther Party [Reconsidered]*; Black Classic Press.

Adogame, A (2011); "Introduction." In A. Adogame (Ed), *Who is Afraid of the Holy Ghost: Pentecostalism and Globalization in Africa and Beyond*; Africa World Press.

Afrika, L (2013); Dr Llaila Afrika We Are Different; http://m.youtube.com/watch?v=r6aaP6Ynoj4, accessed in May 2014.

Albert, M (2004); *Parecon: Life After Capitalism*; Verso

Alexander, M (2011); *The New Jim Crow: Mass Incarceration in the Age of Colorblindness*; The New Press.

Aptheker, H (1996); "Maroons Within the Present Limits of the United States." In R. Price (Ed), *Maroon Societies: Rebel*

Slave Communities in the Americas; The John Hopkins University Press.

Asante, M. K (2003); "The Afrocentric Idea." In A. Mazama (Ed), *The Afrocentric Paradigm*; Africa World Press, Inc.

Asante, M. K (2013); "Afrocentricity Imagination and Action." In V. Lal (Ed), *Afrocentricity Imagination and Action*; Multiversity & Citizens International.

Ashby, M (2003); *Sacred Sexuality: Ancient Egyptian Tantric Yoga The Neterian Guide to Love, Sexuality, Marriage, Relationships and the Secrets of Sexual Energy Cultivation, Sublimation, and Spiritual Enlightenment*; Sema Institute of Yoga.

Avineri, S (1968); *The Social & Political Thoughts of Karl Marx*; Cambridge University Press.

Balibar, E, Wallerstein, I (1991); *Race, Nation, Class: Ambiguous Identities*; Verso.

Baudrillard, J (2012); *Simulacra and Simulation*; The University Press.

Bauman, Z (2016); *Liquid Modernity*; Polity Press.

Bauman, Z (2003); *Identity Conversations with Benedetto Vecchi*; Polity Press.

Ben-Jochannan, Y (2002); *The Need for a Black Bible*; Black Classic Press.

Bey, M (2020); *Anarcho-Blackness: Notes Toward a Black Anarchism*; AK Press.

Blackburn, R (1988); *The Overthrow of Colonial Slavery 1776-1848*; Verso Books.

Brandchaft, B, Doctors, S, and Sorter, D (2010); *Toward an Emancipatory Psychoanalysis: Brandchaft's Intersubjective Vision*; Routledge.

Brown, F, Driver, S and Briggs, C (2014); *The Brown-Driver-Briggs Hebrew and English Lexicon*; Hendrickson Publishers.

Buber, M (2008); *I and Thou*; Simon & Schuster.

Callinicos, A (2003); *An Anti-Capitalist Manifesto*; Blackwells Publishing Ltd.

Chittick, W (1989); *The Sufi Path of Knowledge*; State University of New York Press.

Chiu, C-Y, Leung, A. K-Y. & Hong, Y-Y (2011); "Cultural Processes: An Overview." In A. K-Y. Leung, C-Y Chiu & Y-Y Hong (Eds), *Cultural Processes A Social Psychological Perspective*; Cambridge University Press.

Churton, T (2015); *Gnostic Mysteries of Sex: Sophia the Wild One and Erotic Christianity*; Inner Traditions.

Collins, J (2006); *Good to Great and the Social Sectors: A Monograph to Accompany Good to Great*; Random House Business.

Collins, J (2020); *Good to Great*; [ONLINE] Available at: https://www.audible.co.uk/webplayer?asin=147359202X&contentDeliveryType=SinglePartBook&ref_=a_minerva_cloudplayer_147359202X&overrideLph=false&initialCPLaunch=true. [Accessed 07/12/2023].

Collins, J & Porras, J. I (2005); *Built to Last: Successful Habits of Visionary Companies*; Random House Business Books.

Cone, J. H (2012); "Theology's great sin: silence in the face of white supremacy." In *The Cambridge Companion to Black Theology*, eds. Dwight N. Hopkins and Edward P. Antonio; Cambridge University Press.

Cone, J. H (2018); *Black Theology and Black Power: Fiftieth Anniversary Edition*; Orbis Books.

Cone, J. H (2020); *A Black Theology of Liberation: 50th Anniversary Edition*; Orbis Books.

Davis, A (2003); *Are Prisons Obsolete?*; Seven Stories Press.

Davis, D (1984); *Slavery and Human Progress*; Oxford University Press.

Degnbol-Martinussen, J, Engberg-Pedersen, P (2005) *Aid: Understanding International Development Cooperation*. London: Zed Book Ltd.

Diop, A (1991); *Civilization or Barbarism*; Lawrence Hill Books.

Douglas, K. B (1999); *Sexuality and the Black Church: A Womanist Perspective*; Orbis Books.

Durkheim, E (2014) *The Rules of Sociological Method: And Selected Texts on Sociology and its Method*. New York: Free Press.

Durkheim, E, Mauss, M (2009); *Primitive Classification*; Taylor & Francis.

Ehrman, B. D (2003); *Lost Scriptures: Books that Did Not Make It into the New Testament*; Oxford University Press, Inc.

Elias, N (2014) *The Civilizing Process*. Oxford: Blackwell Publishing.

Engberg-Pedersen, P, Gibbon, P, Raikes, P, Udsholt, L (1996) *Limits of Adjustment in Africa: The Effects of Economic Liberalization, 1986-94*. Suffolk: James Curry Ltd., Heinemann, Reed Publishing.

Engels, F (1947); *Anti-Dühring Herr Eugen Dühring's Revolution in Science*; Progress Publishers.

Foner, P (2002); *The Black Panther Speaks*; Da Capo Press.

Fanon, F (1964); *Toward the African Revolution*; Grove Press.

Fanon, F (1965) *A Dying Colonialism*; Grove Press.

Fanon, F (1969); *The Wretched of the Earth*; Penguin Books.

Fanon, F (2008) *Black Skin, White Masks*; Pluto Press.

Feuerstein, G (1998); *Tantra: The Path of Ecstasy*; Shambhala Publications, Inc.

Foucault, M (1998) *The History of Sexuality Vol. 1: The Will to Knowledge*; Penguin Books.

Foxe, J (2001); *Foxe's Book of Martyrs*; Bridge-Logos Publishing.

Franco, J. L (1996); "Maroons and Slave Rebellions in the Spanish Territories." In R. Price (Ed), *Maroon Societies: Rebel Slave Communities in the Americas*; The John Hopkins University Press.

Freeden, M (2013); "The Morphological Analysis of Ideology." In M. Freeden, L. T. Sargent, and M. Stears (Eds), *The Oxford Handbook of Political Ideologies*; Oxford University Press.

Gahlin, L (2007); *Egypt: Gods, Myths and Religion*; Anness Publishing Ltd.

Gentles-Peart, K (2016); *Romance with Voluptuousness: Caribbean Women and Thick Bodies in the US*; University of Nebraska Press.

Gilroy, P (1999); *The Black Atlantic: Modernity and Double Consciousness*; Verso.

Gladwell, M (2002); *The Tipping Point: How Little Things Can Make a Big Difference New Edition*; Abacus.

Gladwell, M (2009); *Outliers: the Story of Success*; Penguin Books.

Gleick, J (1998); *Chaos: The Amazing Science of the Unpredictable*; Vintage Books.

Goldman, E (1911); *Marriage and Love*; Mother Earth Publishing Association.

Gordon, L (2012); "Requim on a Life Well Lived: In Memory of Fanon." In N. Gibson (Ed), *Living Fanon: Global Perspectives*; Palgrave Macmillan.

Grady-Willis, W. A (2005); "The Black Panther Party: State Repression and Political Prisoners." In C. E. Jones (Ed), *The Black Panther Party [Reconsidered]*; Black Classic Press.

Gramsci, A (1971); *Antonio Gramsci: Selections from the Prison Notebooks*; Lawrence &Wishart Ltd.

Graves-Brown, C (2010); *Dancing for Hathor: Women in Ancient Egypt*; Continuum Books.

Greene, R (2004); *The Art of Seduction*; Profile Books.

Grinker, R, Lubkemann, S, Steiner, C (2010); *Perspectives on Africa: A Reader in Culture, History, and Representation Second Edition*; Blackwell Publishing Ltd.

Hardt, M, Negri, A (2000) *Empire*; Harvard University Press.

Harman, C (1999); *Economics of the Madhouse*; Bookmarks Publications Ltd.

Harrison, L (2002); "On Cultural Nationalism." In P. Foner (Ed), *The Black Panther Speaks*; Da Capo Press.

Harvey, D (2006); *Limits to Capital*; Verso Book.

Hawass, Z (2006); *The Royal Tombs of Egypt*; Thames & Hudson Ltd.

Hayes, F. W, III, Francis, K. A, III (2005); "'All Power to the People': The Political Thought of Huey P. Newton and The Black Panther Party." In C. E. Jones (Ed), *The Black Panther Party [Reconsidered]*; Black Classic Press.

Herring, G (2006); *Christianity: From the Early Church to the Enlightenment*; Continuum International Publishing Group.

Heywood, A (2017); *Political Ideologies: An Introduction*; Palgrave.

Hill, N (2004); *Think and Grow Rich Revised and Expanded by Dr Arthur R. Pell*; Vermillion London.

Hudson, M (2021) *Super Imperialism: The Economic Strategy of American Empire Third Edition*. Dresden: ISLET-Verlag.

Ibn Katheer Dimashqi, H (2006); *Book of the End: Great Trials and Tribulations*; Maktaba Dar-us-Salam.

Imseis, A (2010); "Speaking Truth to Power: On Edward Said and the Palestinian Freedom Struggle." In A. Iskandar and H. Rustom (Eds), *Edward Said: A Legacy of Emancipation and Representation*; University of California Press.

Intelexual Media (2023); *A Short History of Masturbation*; [ONLINE] Available at: https://www.youtube.com/watch?v=0aoY6Ihjips. [Accessed 29/11/2023].

Islam, S (2024); *The Revolutionary Anti-Imperialism of the Apostle Paul: Constructive Considerations for a Ghetto Theology Black Divinity Series Vol 1*; Divinity Black People Ltd

Jackson, S. A (2009); *Islam and the Problem of Black Suffering*; Oxford University Press.

Jacobs, M (1992); *Key Figures in Counselling and Psychotherapy: Sigmund Freud*; Sage Publications Ltd.

Johnson, O. A (2005); "Explaining the Demise of The Black Panther Party: The Role o Internal Factions." In C. E. Jones (Ed), *The Black Panther Party [Reconsidered]*; Black Classic Press.

Jones, W. R (1998); *Is God a White Racist? A Preamble to Black Theology*; Beacon Press.

Josephus, F (2013); *The Works of Josephus: New Updated Edition*; Hendrickson Publishers.

Karenga, M (1989); *Introduction to Black Studies*; University of Sankore Press.

Katz, A (2008); *The Holocaust: Where Was God? An Inquiry into the Biblical Roots of Tragedy*; Burning Bush Press.

Keen, D (2012); *Useful Enemies: When Waging Wars is More Important than Winning Them*; Yale University Press.

Khalfe, A. (2019); *An Outpouring of Subtleties upon the Pearl of Oneness Volume 1: Divinity*; Sunni Publications.

Killah Priest (1996); "B.I.B.L.E." In: *Liquid Swords* [CD]; Geffen/MCA.

King, M. L, Jr (1986); *A Testament of Hope*; HarperCollins Publishers.

King, M. L, Jr (1992); *I Have A Dream; Writings and Speeches That Changed the World*; HarperCollins Publishing.

Koester, C. R (2014); *Revelation: A New Translation with Introduction and Commentary*; Yale University Press.

Koestler, A (1976); *The Thirteenth Tribe*; Random House, Inc.

Kolawole, M. E. M (1997); *Womanism and African Consciousness*; African World Press.

Kropotkin, P (2002); *Anarchism*; Dover Publications Inc.

Kropotkin, P (2006); *Mutual Aid: A Factor of Evolution*; Dover Publications Inc.

Kumar, D (2012); *Islamophobia and the Politics of Empire*; Haymarket Books.

Lady Gaga (2009); *Poker Face (Official Music Video).* [ONLINE] Available at: https://www.youtube.com/watch?v=bESGLojNYSo. [Accessed 31/12/2023].

Lenin, V (1968); *V. I. Lenin Selected Works*; Lawrence and Wishart Ltd.

Lenin, V (2010); *Imperialism: The Highest Stage of Capitalism*; Penguin Books.

Lenin, V (2014); *State and Revolution*; Haymarket Books. Square Press, Inc.

Lenin, V (2020); *What Is to Be Done? Burning Questions of Our Movement*; Science Marxiste.

lil' bill (2023); *How Black Elites LIE to Us*; [ONLINE] Available at: https://www.youtube.com/watch?v=Uu-X_E8cwaA. [Accessed 29/11/2023].

Littlewood, R (2006); *Pathology and Identity: The Work of Mother Earth in Trinidad*; Cambridge University Press.

Lizokin-Eyzenberg, E & Shir, P (2021); *Hebrew Insights From Revelation.* Israel: Jewish Studies for Christians.

Luxemburg, R (2004); *The Rosa Luxemburg Reader*; The Monthly Review Press.

Lyotard, J (1986); *The Postmodern Condition: A Report on Knowledge*; Manchester University Press.

MacCulloch, D (2010); *A History of Christianity*; Penguin Random House.

Mackenzie-Grieve, A (1968); *The Last Years of the English Slave Trade Liverpool 1750-1807*; Frank Cass & co. Ltd.

Malatesta, E (1922); *At the Café: Conversations on Anarchism*; KDP Amazon Publishing.

Malcioln, J (1996); *The African Origins of Modern Judaism*; Africa World.

Marx, K (1986); *Capital Volume I*; Lawrence &Wishart Ltd.

Marx, K (1958); *Selected Works vol 3*; Foreign Languages Publishing House.

Maxwell, M (1998); *Revelation: Doubleday Bible Commentary*; Bantam Doubleday Dell Publication Group, Inc.

M'Bantu, A, Muller, G (2013); *The Ancient Black Hebrews and Arabs*; Pomegranate Publishing.

McHugo, J (2019); *A Concise History of Sunnis & Shi'is*. London: Saqi Books.

McRobbie, A (2008); *Pornographic Permutations*; Routledge.

Meiu, G. P (2011); "'Mombasa morans': embodiment, sexuality and Samburu men in Kenya." In S. Tamale (Ed), *African Sexualities: A Reader*; Pambazuka Press.

Meyer, M, W (1992); *The Gospel of Thomas: The Hidden Saying of Jesus*; Harper.

Moltmann, J (1993); *Theology of Hope: On the Ground and Implications of a Christian Eschatology*. Minnesota: Fortress Press.

Mellino, M (2011); "Notes from the Underground, Fanon, Africa, and the Poetics of the Real." In *Living Fanon: Global Perspectives* (Ed). Nigel C. Gibson; Palgrave Macmillan.

Muhammad, E (1965); *Message to the Blackman of America*; Muhammad's Temple of Islam No. 2.

Muhammad, E (1973); *The Fall of America*; Muhammad's Temple of Islam No. 2.

Newton, H (2002); *The Huey P. Newton Reader*; Seven Stories Press.

Nkrumah, K (2006); *Class Struggle in Africa*; Panaf Books.

Nkrumah, K (2009); *Consciencism Philosophy and Ideology for De-Colonization*; Monthly Review Press.

Nkrumah, K (2022); *Neo-Colonialism: The Last Stage of Imperialism*; African People's Conference.

Nye, J S, Jr (2004); *Soft Power: The Means to Success in World Politics*; Public Affairs Books.

Nzegwu, N (2011); "'Osunality' (or African eroticism)." In S. Tamale (Ed), *African Sexualities: A Reader*; Pambazuka Press.

Patterson, O (1996); "Slavery and Slave Revolts: A Sociohistorical Analysis of the First Maroon War, 1665-1740." In R. Price (Ed), *Maroon Societies: Rebel Slave Communities in the Americas*; The John Hopkins University Press.

Philo (2016); *The Works of Philo: Complete and Unabridged New Updated Edition*; Hendrickson Publishers Marketing, LLC.

Raja, M (2020); *Decolonizing Literary Theory: Some Tentative Thoughts | Zahiriyya and Bataniyya Philosophy*; [ONLINE] Available at: https://www.youtube.com/watch?v=Ez7UZUCM8wo. [Accessed 06/12/2023]

Rand, N. T (1994); "New Perspectives in Metapsychology: Cryptic Mourning and Secret Love." In N. T. Rand (Ed), *The Shell and the Kernel*; University of Chicago Press.

Rand, N. T (1994); "Secrets and Posterity: The Theory of the Transgenerational Phantom." In N. T. Rand (Ed), *The Shell and the Kernel*; University of Chicago Press.

Roberts, A (2011); *Evolution The Human Story*; Dorling Kindersley Limited.

Roberts, J. D (2012); "Dignity and destiny: black reflections on eschatology." In *The Cambridge Companion to Black Theology*, eds. Dwight N. Hopkins and Edward P. Antonio. Cambridge: Cambridge University Press.

Rogers, K (1976); *The Gambler*. [ONLINE] Available at: https://www.youtube.com/watch?v=7hx4gdlfamo. [Accessed 31/12/2023].

Rowland, C (1985); *Christian Origins: An Account of the Setting and Character of the most Important Messianic Sect of Judaism*; SPCK.

Said, E (2003) *Orientalism*. London: Penguin Books.

Saraswati, S (2012); *Kundalini Tantra*; Yoga Publications Trust.

Sardar, Z, Abrams, I (2012); *Introducing Chaos: A Graphic Guide*; Icon Book Ltd.

Schimek, J-G (2011); *Memory, Myth, and Seduction: Unconscious Fantasy and the Interpretive Process*; Routledge.

Seale, B (2002); "The Ten-Point Platform and Program of the Black Panther Party." In P. Foner (Ed), *The Black Panther Speaks*; Da Capo Press.

Seleem, R (2004); *The Egyptian Book of Life*; Watkins Publishing London.

Seligman, C. G (1966); *Races of Africa*; Oxford University Press.

Sheller, M (2012); *Citizenship From Below: Erotic Agency and Caribbean Freedom*; Duke University Press.

Singh, N. P (2005); "The Black Panthers and the 'Undeveloped Country' of the Left." In C. E. Jones (Ed), *The Black Panther Party [Reconsidered]*; Black Classic Press.

Skousen, M (2017); *The Big Three in Economics: Adam Smith, Karl Marx, and John Maynard Keynes*; Routledge.

Smif-N-Wessun (1995); "Home Sweet Home." In *Dah Shinin'* [CD]. New York: Wreck Records, Nervous, Inc.

Smif-N-Wessun (1995); "PNC." In *Dah Shinin'* [CD]. New York: Wreck Records, Nervous, Inc.

Snoop Doggy Dogg (1994); *Doggystyle*; Death Row Records.

St. Augustine (1958); *City of God*; Bantam Doubleday Dell Publishing Group, Inc.

Stourton, E (2005); *In the Footsteps of Saint Paul*; Hodder Headlin Ltd.

Strong, J (1990); *The New Strong's Exhaustive Concordance of the Bible*; Thomas Nelson Publishers.

Strachey, J (1936); *The Theory and Practice of Socialism*; Victor Gúllancz Ltd.

The Holy Bible: King James Version (2002); Michigan: Zondervan.

The Holy Qur'an: Maulana Muhammad Ali Translation (2002); Ohio: Ahmadiyya Anjuman Isha'at Islam Lahore Inc.

Torok, M (1994); "The Illness of Mourning and the Fantasy of the Exquisite Corpse." In N. T. Rand (Ed), *The Shell and the Kernel*; University of Chicago Press.

Turman, E. M (2018); "Heaven and Hell in African American Theology." In *The Oxford Handbook of African American Theology*, eds. Katie G. Cannon and Anthony B. Pinn; Oxford University Press.

Turner, L (2011); "Fanon and the Biopolitics of Torture: Contextualizing Psychological Practices as Tools of War." In N. Gibson (Ed), *Living Fanon: Global Perspectives*; Palgrave Macmillan.

Tyldesley, J (2011); *The Penguin Book of Myths & Legends of Ancient Egypt*; Penguin Books.

Umoja, A. O (2005); "Set Our Warriors Free: The Legacy of The Black Panther Party and Political Prisoners." In C. E. Jones (Ed), *The Black Panther Party [Reconsidered]*; Black Classic Press.

Van Loon, H (1960); *The Story of Mankind*; Washington Square Press, Inc.

Vanee, L (2023); *End the Genocide* [ONLINE] Available at: https://www.facebook.com/reel/1584869658715687. [Accessed 17/12/2023].

Wacquant, L (2016) "Bourdieu, Foucault, and the Penal State in the Neoliberal Era." In D. Zamora & M. C. Behrent (Eds), *Foucault and Neoliberalism*. Cambridge: Polity Press.

Watterson, B (2013); *Women in Ancient Egypt*; Amberley Publishing.

Williams, D. S (1993); *Sisters in the Wilderness: The Challenge of Womanist God-Talk*; Orbis Books.

Williams, D. S (2011); "Black Theology and Womanist Theology." In D. N. Hopkins & E. P. Antonio (Eds), *The

Cambridge Companion to Black Theology; Cambridge University Press.

Williams, J (1928); *Hebrewisms of West Africa From the Nile to the Niger with the Jews*; Africa Tree Press.

X, M (1968); *The Autobiography of Malcolm X*; Penguin Books.

X, M (2004); *Why I am Not an American*; Citizens International.